Giles Badger Stebbins

The American protectionist's manual

Giles Badger Stebbins

The American protectionist's manual

ISBN/EAN: 9783337277765

Printed in Europe, USA, Canada, Australia, Japan

Cover: Foto ©Suzi / pixelio.de

More available books at **www.hansebooks.com**

THE

AMERICAN PROTECTIONIST'S

MANUAL.

PROTECTION TO HOME INDUSTRY

ESSENTIAL TO NATIONAL INDEPENDENCE AND TO THE WELL-BEING OF THE PEOPLE.

BRITISH FREE TRADE

A DELUSION AND A PERIL.

BY

GILES B. STEBBINS,
DETROIT, MICH.

DETROIT:
THORNDIKE NOURSE.
1883.

CONTENTS.

CHAPTER I.

INTRODUCTORY. THE TARIFF QUESTION SIMPLE.—Tariff revision. How more important than how much. How long shall protective duties last? *Ad valorem* rates not best 1

CHAPTER II.

WHAT IS PROTECTION? WHAT IS FREE TRADE?—Protection not a "Chinese wall" or a panacea 9

CHAPTER III.

VARIED INDUSTRY A HELP TO CIVILIZATION 13

CHAPTER IV.

PROTECTION ABROAD. EUROPE NOT FREE TRADE . . . 19

CHAPTER V

BRITISH FREE TRADE A DELUSION.—Monopoly of all markets. "A free trade tariff" a false claim. Reaction against free trade in England. British intermeddling. The Cobden Club. We must protest. English contributors to free trade funds in New York. Early fears of our manufactures. Hands off! 24

CHAPTER VI.

THE FREE TRADE FALSEHOOD THAT A PROTECTIVE TARIFF IS A TAX ON THE CONSUMER REFUTED.—Alexander Hamilton. Cottons. Silks. Woolens and wool. Honorable ignorance. Cheap woolens. British factory life. British shoddy. The poor farmer and his blankets. Flannels, etc. Iron and steel. Steel rails, nails, saws, axes, cutlery, salt, lumber. Loose and reckless assertions. "Consolations of the protected farmer;" a Canadian view. Chemicals. Farmers the greatest monopolists, the nonsense of it 47

CHAPTER VII.

A TARIFF FOR REVENUE ONLY, TAXES THE CONSUMER. Duties and prices. The old store and the new. A tariff like a levee or a fence. Why do we not export manufactures largely? 85

CHAPTER VIII.

SOME FREE TRADE FALLACIES ANSWERED.—"Protection fetters trade." "Hotbed growth." "Buy in the cheapest market." "Cheap foreign articles are clear gain." "Balance of trade fallacious" 93

CHAPTER IX.

PROTECTION AND THE FARMER.—Old time experiences—selling cheap and buying dear. Wise industrial policy needed for successful farming. Rich lands exhausted. Farm and factory neighbors and allies. Purchasing power of farmers. Cheap transportation. Address of E. B. Ward. The Western protectionist and the Cobden Club man; Dudley on Mongredien. Duties on farm products. Grain and provisions; exports and home market. A healthy equilibrium. Foreign markets uncertain. How protection protects farmers. A farmer's statement . . . 99

CHAPTER X.

WAGES AND PROTECTION.—Wages and costs, here and in England, etc. Savings Bank deposits; seven to one. Woman's elevation. Wages in Newark, Paisley and the Clyde ship-yards. J. W. Hinton. Comparative taxes. Statements at New York and Chicago Tariff Conventions . . 130

CHAPTER XI.

OPINIONS OF EMINENT MEN 153

CHAPTER XII.

COMMON INTEREST, NOT SECTIONAL OR CLASS JEALOUSY.—New England industries. The new South. A Western view 163

CHAPTER XIII.

OUR HISTORY TEACHES THE BENEFITS OF PROTECTION.—Protective tariffs pay surest and best revenue 179

CHAPTER XIV

FOREIGN COMMERCE—AMERICAN SHIPS. CONCLUSION . 188

CHAPTER I.

INTRODUCTORY—THE TARIFF QUESTION SIMPLE.

We have no brief compendium for popular use, including a broad discussion of protection to home industry, criticism of free trade assertions and theories, and exposure of the delusion and peril of British free trade. Large volumes and valuable essays and tracts have had wide reading, but a condensed manual is wanted. This book aims to supply that want, and to present the leading principles and facts on this great question in such compass as to be readable and useful in the homes of the people, in libraries, and as a help in discussions. A generation has passed away since the great discussion of the tariff in the days of Henry Clay and Horace Greeley, and there are now many who want information to gain more positive and clear views and opinions. There are protectionists and free traders, equally sincere and earnest in their opposite opinions, yet wishing more light. A question so important and prominent deserves careful thought and serious attention. The statements of this work are offered as helps to all these classes. Its plain criticisms expose the methods and aims of leading free trade advocates, and cut across the grain of strong prejudices, but they do not impugn the honesty of well-meaning and sincere free traders.

Many of our college professors and text-books favor free trade. These teachers often lack practical knowledge of the world, and are captivated by fine English theories, which are easy to accept, and save the trouble of studying the facts of our industrial history, as given by Carey, Elder, Thompson, Bowen, Kelley and other able Americans, or like facts and ideas in the writings of Sir Edward Sullivan, Sir Matthew Byles, Thiers, Frederick List and other eminent foreigners. But there are signs of a change. In Yale and elsewhere students are calling for light on protection to American industry.

The tariff question is supposed by many to be abstruse and difficult, a labyrinth of facts and figures to which none can find a clue except the few who can give it long and patient study. This is a mistake; the principles involved are plain and simple. It is thought of as a dry matter of dollars and dimes in the national treasury, and of profit and loss to great capitalists; or as a soulless thing galvanized into life now and then as the war-cry of a political campaign. It is full of vital interest and comes home to the daily life of the people. Political economy and social science should be more studied. Surely what pertains so closely to the peaceful industries which so largely fill our time should be as well understood as the poor quarrels of old kings with their ministers or mistresses, or the wars that have worse than wasted the strength of the human race.

A family pays special regard to the interests of its own members, while not oppressing or abusing others: a nation is a great family. A family earns its own expenses, or more, or decays; a nation sells as much as it buys or decays. This is "the balance of trade." When any one can show how a family can earn $900 and pay out $1,000 yearly, and still prosper, we may see how a nation can export $90,000,000 and import $100,000,000 yearly, and not grow poor.

A family, the members of which toil and care for each other, cannot be expected to admit others, who do not share these cares, into all its privileges and immunities; and none complain if its first and nearest aim is to see that its own members are well employed and in a way to independence. A nation, whose people have cleared its lands, built its mills and shops and mechanism, opened its beds of ores and coal, and are paying its debts and taxes, cannot be expected to admit foreigners, who have no share in these tasks or burthens, to its markets on equal terms with its own citizens. A tariff is a means of asking them to pay reasonably for the privilege of bringing in their products, and at the same time of building up home industries, and giving employ and independence to the people. Nothing abstruse or complicated in all this.

We are to look at this protective tariff matter as it is practiced now, and as it now affects people and nations, especially our own country—going back to the past for such facts as may help to comprehend the present. In the dark ages of personal government by royal despots exclusive privileges of making, or dealing in, salt, woolens, etc., were farmed out to favorites. The people had no rights, their interest was not counted, the only question was, how much extortion will they bear?

Wealth was won by the sword, and the rude loom and the poor tillage of the soil was left to women and slaves, and to the lame and halt not fit to be soldiers. Duties were levied, now and then, on exports or imports, with no thought or care for anything save to raise money. Tariffs for revenue only, advocated by modern free traders, are relics of the barbaric ignorance of those dark days when the artificer was despised and the robber warrior exalted.

Then came slowly a recognition of the national importance of building up great industries, and legislation to that end. England, for instance, had a rigid system of tariffs for centuries, highly protective and with special prohibitions such as no country to-day would enact. The influence of legislation on the people fortunately enters more into the governmental acts of all civilized nations now than in the past, and especially is that the case in this republican country. By that test is this matter to be tried. If our protective tariff system works for the benefit of favored manufacturers, giving wealthy capitalists unjust monopolies and privileges at the cost of their employees and of the people, helping to enrich the few at the expense of the many, it is not fit to live a day. If it helps to build up great and varied domestic industries; to employ labor at higher wages than elsewhere; to perfect and cheapen the products of our mills by a healthy competition; to open a larger and better home market for our farmers; to develop our great natural resources; to furnish revenue to our government; to help our financial and industrial independence, and to enrich and enlarge the daily thought and life of the people, it should be sustained. All these benefits, it is claimed, result from it.

TARIFF REVISION.

The tariff framed in 1861—largely by the patient care of Hon. Justin S. Morrill, U. S. S., of Vermont, a man of eminent capacity and integrity—and modified after the close of the war, in 1870, has done excellent service, helping us through war and world-wide business panic. During this time we have reached a magnitude of home production on the farm, in the factory, and in domestic and foreign trade, increasing beyond like growth in any other country or any previous increase in the same time at home. As changes in our condition seemed to call for its revision, a tariff commission was chosen by the President in 1882, made up of nine practical and able men, outside of Congress, who were to investigate the whole matter and report facts and opinions to Congress, their report (which was made December 4, 1882, and is of permanent value) to be information and advisory basis for final legislation by that body, that its work might be broad and comprehensive, so well done as to stand for a term of years, to avoid the trouble and disaster of frequent changes and fragmentary tariff tinkering, and give that stability which we need for safety in industrial enterprises. Such revision was approved and asked for by leading producers and manufacturers. During the sessions of the Forty-sixth Congress 257 large manufacturing companies and 80,867 workmen sent petitions to that body asking the appointment of such commissioners. It is not in the scope of this work to comment on the action of Congress in the tariff bill passed in the last days of their session just closed. This much only can be said : Any changes, either of reduction or increase, which kept the idea of just protection in view were wise ; any changes ignoring it were unwise.

HOW MORE IMPORTANT THAN HOW MUCH.

The German revenue from customs duties, a little less in amount than the English, is levied by a protective tariff. Such a tariff *discriminates in favor of the people of the country where it is framed.* A tariff for revenue only *discriminates against them and in favor of foreigners.* This it does by allowing free competition in the products of their industry, and taxing foreign products which they cannot produce or compete with. Two tariff schedules might be framed for a country, both aiming to raise the same sum for revenue, yet the one might be a benefit and the other a fearful injury. The how is more important than the how much, and *a tariff for revenue only is the danger and calamity to be avoided.* A few years ago Professor Perry gave his "revenue tariff" scheme as follows :

"I would throw off at a st.. ninety per cent. of all the articles taxed in our present tariff. I would remit the duties on the rest to that point at which the most revenue would come in, with the least interference with the industries of the people."

By duties on fifteen or twenty articles he proposed to raise a revenue of $150,000,000 yearly, and said :

"Why, last year we realized on tea and coffee, sugar and molasses, wines and spirits, tobacco and snuff—four classified articles—$63,595,000."

To impose high duties on such articles as we do not and cannot produce or manufacture, and low duties, if any, on our iron, woolens, cotton, etc., is his scheme and that of other free trade revenue reformers. It is the British scheme, and it is a fine device to take the tax from the products of British manufacturers imported into this country and levy it on the comforts and necessaries of the American farmer and workingman. It is a premium or discrimination in favor of foreign manufacturers and foreign pauper wages, and against our own manufacturers and farmers and better paid workmen. For a time more revenue might be raised, but soon disaster and loss of revenue would follow. Frame the tariff with fit duties for protection and revenue on such articles as we can make or produce, and admit foreign products—tea, coffee, etc.—which we cannot produce, free of duty, and the sure revenue is easily raised amidst permanent prosperity. The facts of our history verify this statement.

AD VALOREM DUTIES NOT BEST.

Sometimes such duties may be necessary, but usually specific rates are best—so much per yard or pound, etc.—or most honest and not easily evaded. A late report of Mr. Martin, a special treasury agent, says:

"Since the passage of the act of June 22, 1874, commonly called the 'Anti-Moiety Act,' the undervaluation of all kinds of imported merchandise has steadily increased from year to year until at the present time its proportions are enormous. The reports from agents sent abroad to examine into the subject show that nearly all classes of goods paying ad valorem duties exported from various countries to the United States are undervalued. More particularly is this the case with goods consigned by the foreign manufacturers to their agents in this country. The practice of consigning goods has grown to such proportions that there has been absolutely no foreign market value for many articles imported, as there are no sales of such goods in the open market, the American merchants being compelled to purchase from the agent of the manufacturer to whom goods are consigned. Investigation has shown that upon the advice of the agent foreign manufacturers often invoice consigned goods far below the cost of production. It is estimated that less than 40 per cent. of the 60 per cent. ad valorem duty on silk is collected in consequence of the undervaluation of that article.

Velvets, plushes, laces, embroideries, edgings and like articles have been reported as systematically undervalued by the foreign manufacturers, many of whom openly admit that they invoice their goods to this country at lower values than they do to other countries."

Iron and steel are undervalued in like manner. The low rates at which these goods are invoiced do not benefit the American customer, for the consignee advances his price to their real value. The larger part of the importing in New York is done through these agents, almost always foreigners. An Englishman or a German will rent a small chamber on Broadway and sell goods by sample; he pays no taxes, is not a citizen, has no interest for us, and is a free trader of course. The regular importing merchant, who would do a more honorable business, suffers from the number of these agencies.

HOW LONG SHALL PROTECTIVE DUTIES LAST?

In England they lasted for centuries, and a strong feeling is growing there in opposition to the present free trade policy. In other European countries such duties exist to-day. Evidently we are not near their end in this new country. They are not evils to be put aside, or burthens to be cast off as soon as possible, but benefits to be maintained so long as necessary. Suppose all wars ended and all national debts paid (and this happy consummation is in the distance) the necessity for new industries, to meet the growing and complex wants of a civilization higher than we can imagine, would exist. Either by protective duties, or by some system inspired by the same idea, nations would still encourage their own producers.

This book is not an effort either to maintain or to change existing duties, but to uphold and illustrate the idea of protection as the inspiring soul of tariff legislation.

The aim is to put within reach of all a manual or compendium of an American policy of protection to home industry.

CHAPTER II.

WHAT IS PROTECTION?—WHAT IS FREE TRADE?

Protection to home industry is a practical fact; it is the policy of almost every civilized nation, and is as firmly established among these nations to-day as ever. It is not a relic of barbarism, but an inspiring and guiding element in our highest industrial civilization.

Free trade is a theory, its practice unknown in any civilized land. Only savages are absolutely free traders, and they have no trade.

The idea of protection is that each government should encourage the industry and skill of its people, and the development of the natural resources of its territory, and that, to this end customs-duties on foreign imports should be so levied as to prevent the free importation of such articles as can be made, or produced, at home, and also to furnish needed government revenue. Duties thus levied, it is claimed, so encourage and protect home manufactures, and home labor and skill, that those manufactures grow solid, the workman gets varied employ, and the common good is advanced.

It is indeed difficult to find, in any country, great industries which have grown up under free trade.

PROTECTION NOT PROHIBITION OR A PANACEA.

Instead of building up a "Chinese wall," our national experience shows that a large and healthy foreign trade —both exports and imports—grows up with protective duties, which help to solid wealth at home as safe basis for domestic and foreign commerce. Our tariff regulates, but does not prevent, imports; it invigorates and fructifies our home domain steadily and constantly, while every approach to free trade gives us the deluge and then the dearth.

Protection is not a panacea, good against crop failures, bad business management or extravagance, but a powerful element in the conservation and development of national resources and of personal skill and power. There can be no inflexible standard of duties; rates good for one country may be too high or too low for another, and each nation must consider its rates of interest, and wages and revenue needs, and so shape its tariff as to give its people fair scope for competition with others.

Free trade is absolutely unrestricted international intercourse; free exports and imports without custom houses. It does not exist outside of savage lands. Great Britain, its professed apostle and propagandist, has, as will be shown, but a deceptive and fragmentary approach to this theory. It has been styled "A Science based on Assumptions," and its advocates abound in metaphysical theories, and in strange notions that truth can be got out of abstruse assertions unsustained by facts. Plainly enough, if political economy is to be of any value, we want the light of facts and experience as a guide to correct ideas. More historic truths and careful statements touching industry and trade—figures, dates, causes and results—can be found in a single volume of Henry C. Carey than in a score of standard free trade books. *Rich in assertion and unsustained theory, but poor in facts,* must be the verdict as to free trade writers.

M. Chevalier, an able French statesman, well said:

"Every nation owes it to itself to seek the establishment of diversification in the pursuits of its people. * * * It is not an abuse of power, but the doing of a positive duty by governments, so to act at each epoch in the progress of a nation as to favor the taking possession of all the branches of industry whose acquisition is authorized in the nature of things."

Such "taking possession," not by monopoly, but by fair competition, is the aim of a protective policy.

John Stuart Mill says in his Political Economy:

"The superiority of one country over another in a branch of production often arises from having begun it sooner. There may be no inherent advantage or disadvantage on either side, but only a present superiority of skill and experience. A country which has these to acquire may, in other respects, be better adapted to the production than those earlier in the field; and besides, it is a just remark, that nothing has a greater tendency to produce improvement in any branch of production than its trial under a new set of conditions. But it cannot be expected that individuals, at their own cost, should introduce a new manufacture, and bear the burthens of carrying it on until the producers have been educated up to the line of those with whom the processes have become traditional. A PROTECTIVE DUTY, continued for a reasonable time, will sometimes be the least inconvenient mode in which a country can tax itself for the support of such an experiment."

This grants the argument to protection, as a principle, and comes from a free trade writer of eminent ability and character.

To advocate protection for any industry—iron, woolen, wool, etc.—while advocating free trade or tariff for revenue only, on other articles, is not the true way. The interdependence of all industries, and such fair protection as each and all may need, must be the guide and motive of honest and fair action.

Hon. W. H. Calkins, M. C., of Indiana, well said.

"I consider it to be my duty as a representative of the people to protect the labor of this country. I do not care what the product of that labor may be, whether it be pig-iron, or clothing, or sugar, or anything else. I want to protect the laborer in Louisiana just as far and as much as I want to protect the laborer in the iron-mill of Pennsylvania or Indiana, and no further. In my judgment that is all there is in this question. The keystone principle upon which this country rests is that labor is noble. Hence, we should put it in the power of the laborer to get the highest wages obtainable, not only for his own benefit, but that he may support and educate his children to become useful members of society. That is the idea of protection."

Protection does not establish monopoly, but breaks down foreign monopoly by encouraging home competition. It does not aim to benefit one class at the cost of another, or to build up one industry at the expense of another, but to benefit all by a just recognition of the interdependence of all industries. It helps domestic commerce and develops our own resources, and so gives solid basis for a healthy foreign commerce. It defends the weak against the strong, cares for those of our own household, aims to advance the welfare of the working people by opening varied employments at fair wages, and elevates the character of our national life.

The American Free Trade League in New York defines its position as follows :

"We believe in the utmost possible freedom for all citizens of the United States in trade as well as in other relations of life ; but we recognize that absolute freedom of trade must be limited by the revenue necessities of the government, just as absolute freedom in other respects is necessarily limited by government; and therefore the Free Trade League willingly submits to taxation and duties to meet the government necessities ; while it denounces as robbery and tyranny all taxation for the benefit of special classes."

This is free trade and tariff for revenue only, which holds protection as "robbery" to "benefit special classes."

CHAPTER III.

VARIED INDUSTRY A HELP TO BETTER CIVILIZATION.

To look at the policy of a nation only as it may affect wealth in money and other material things is a partial and fragmentary view, not the highest and therefore incomplete. Such wealth is important, but must be gained and used as a means to a high end—national and personal character. The old way of winning wealth was by warlike robbery; the new way is by supremacy in peaceful industry.

An individual will aim to acquire personal independence; equally does a nation,—a great family of millions of individuals,—want national independence. The individual, if wise, seeks such occupation as will give scope to his genius and ennoble his character while he wins daily bread and lays by some savings. The nation should so shape its policy as to give scope to the varied genius of its people and help them to a higher life, while they win its wealth by their toil and skill. Governments personify nations, and should use their power and influence for the best good of all; especially is this the mission and duty of a free government, whose officials are but the chosen and trusted servants of the people.

The wondrous growth of man from savage to civilized life is a development and culture of varied powers of mind and body to meet the many wants and finer tastes of the more perfect being. The savage has a narrow round of simple occupations, few wants easily supplied, thoughts that take in his own tribe but go out beyond in dim confusion. Yet in that lower nature are the germs of a higher, a divine intent ever tends to lift all upward, and at last come the larger range of thought, the more complex occupations, the many wants, the demand for beauty and order and perfectness, which make up civilization and true freedom. The industry of the savage is simple, that of the civilized man is complex. The lesson of history is that varied industry is a product and result of civilization, and that those governments which have done most to encourage it have, in that way, helped to lift the life of their people to a higher level. When government encourages the genius of the people it has the strength of the Eternal Laws on its side. Such encouragement is the idea and aim of protection to home industry.

All the most advanced nations, save England, have a protective policy.

No country can profit so much by diversified industry as the United States, for no other country has such varied advantages and natural resources, with such freedom as quickens the ready and fluent genius of the people.

The protective policy of Russia has helped that empire greatly. Her manufactures increased in value 170 per cent. from 1867 to 1879, reaching near $400,000,000 and employing 750,000,000 workmen. But the shadow of Czarism—personal and irresponsible despotism—chills or corrupts all. Germany has made great progress since the adoption of her Zollverein; but an imperial government with an immense standing army holds a toiling and crowded multitude in subjection. France has gained better results for her people. The revolution of 1789 took the lands, held under the *old regime* by church and state, from the monk and the noblemen for her farmers to hold and till, and this gave new impetus to the skill of her artisans, which the government has wisely encouraged and protected. But France is just entering on an effort for popular government, and has emerged but yesterday from Napoleonic and Bourbon rule and from the waste of war. All these are protective nations, and such are their drawbacks.

England is trying a new experiment,—a professed free trade policy. Already her supremacy is slowly waning. But she has heavy foreign investments, a trade over every sea, built up under her Navigation Laws (now repealed) and by mail contracts and greater than that of any other nation, immense manufactures, profits from funds abroad and from foreign freights and exchanges of money, estimated at from $500,000,000 to $650,000,000 yearly, and manages all with a persistent vigor worthy of admiring respect, differ as we may from a leading feature of her policy. Her trouble and weakness is an island territory too narrow to give scope for the best diversified industry. Her population must be too largely manufacturing, and that dwarfs and cramps the life of the workmen. Her farms cannot feed her factories; she cannot be self-dependent, but must reach out with unrelenting grasp for the world's trade, and for raw material to manufacture. Our cotton she is compelled to have. If it fails a fatal calamity smites her. We are under no such dire necessity of selling it, for we can work it up. Yet we send far the largest share to England as a matter of choice and profit. Doubtless we shall send large future supplies, but great mills, not only in Lowell but in Southern towns, will consume more at home.

The "manifest destiny" of this country is not to be

simply a great agricultural nation, but to build up the richest and most benificent varied industry and commerce in the world.

We cannot have the best farming until we have the best manufacturing, in varied forms and materials, near the farm, each an indispensable help to the growth and perfectness of the other.

Give us both, and the blending of these varied experiencès and vocations, the meeting and mingling of these many life-currents, tinged and shaped by such wide mastery of man over nature's forces and materials, is full of benefit. It is civilization, culture, wealth of soul as well as of purse. To the farmer it is increase of the product of his acres, economy of exchange, work of hand or brain for whatever gift of power or character his children may possess, instant and constant call for a variety of labor, and all the while the thrill of inventive genius pulsing through the serene quiet of his life in the fields, saving it from all narrowness or stagnation, that he may the more enjoy nature's beauty and the better make her forces serve him.

We have exhaustless coal beds, convertible into exhaustless power, and iron, lead, copper and the precious metals, exhaustless also. We have a broad land of varied wealth, cotton and wool and food. With these gifts of a beneficent Creator, we must build up a diversity of occupations, giving complete scope to all powers of body and brain, opening employ to all and helping to a higher civilization.

Thus can we make our labor more productive; elevate its character and make the workman's life larger and richer; save the waste that always follows crude and unskilled processes; and gain that mastery over nature's finer forces and elements which is symmetry, beauty, permanence, strength and delicacy in every product of the skilled artisan, with his genius awakened by the multiform products and processes growing up around him.

We must train our skill, and develop our artistic taste, or we fall behind in the great and peaceful strife of national industries. To be dull laggards in this noble emulation would be sore disaster, keeping us down to poverty of life, few employments, bankruptcy and dependence. Let the settled policy of our government be to protect our industry, and thus develop our great resources and the genius of our people, and we shall show such results in character and wealth and finest skill as the world has never seen. Without such policy we shall grope on in darkness and confusion, the giants trampling the pigmies under foot, and all striking at random to each other's harm.

Under the old conditions in the South, agriculture,— and that almost wholly of one kind, in the cotton field, —was the leading and exclusive occupation. That fact was a blight on the life of the people, and the fortunate hour has come when it is being cured.

In New England there was a wide range of industries, with what results let another tell. At the Fair of the New England Agricultural Society, in Brattleboro, Vt., in 1866, Hon. John A. Andrew, Governor of Massachusetts, eloquently said :

"I desire to attract the observation of this body of intelligent agriculturists to the subject of the diversification of industry, in its relation to the prosperity of the American farmer. I can do little more than remind you that while population has grown beyond a precedent, wealth has advanced beyond population ; that in proportion as our industry has become diversified, our capacity to purchase and enjoy the fruits of the earth has been much more than correspondingly enlarged ; and that the union of the people in a common purpose to develop all their powers, by whatever means, whether intellectual or mechanical, is the secret of their own growth, and the amelioration of the estate of man.

"Better fed, with more fullness and variety; better clad, in more garments, and those more pleasing to the sense of beauty; better sheltered, by houses more commodious, and in styles of more tasteful architecture, and more enduring quality ; with more books and newspapers, and larger public libraries; enjoying incomparably more avenues and better means for traveling, and for transportation of goods; with ampler crops and better prices than ever before—this very Commonwealth does, in its own current history, afford the proof of the advantages of our American aim at the largest conquest over all the domains of industry."

In that "American aim" we can all unite, from Maine to the Gulf, to the Golden Gate on the Pacific coast, and the distant forests "where rolls the Oregon."

Let the reader of the following chapters, while studying facts and statistics bearing on material wealth, find "between the lines" that a protective policy fosters a diversified industry, *and thus helps to enlarge and lift up the life of the people.*

CHAPTER IV.

PROTECTION ABROAD—EUROPE NOT FREE TRADE.

It is supposed by many that the protective policy is contrary to the practice of the great European nations, and that the best European thought is opposed to it. It is the fashion in many of our colleges to assume that free trade is the ideal of the noblest persons and the best minds in the Old World, while protection is a vulgar and selfish matter advocated by those of lesser note and narrower culture. Professor Perry asserts that "to relax commercial systems and not to restrict them is alone in accord with the spirit of the age and the leading commercial nations, the United States alone excepted, have been relaxing their commercial systems." This assertion has little if any proof outside of England. The British Chamber of Commerce declared in 1865 that, "in Russia the importation of foreign articles is practically prevented by a scale of duties higher than any in the world." Some changes were made in 1869, but this same chamber says they "would not lead to any extension of legitimate trade." Austrian duties range from 24 to 67 per cent. Henry C. Carey said the great progress of Germany from poverty to wealth in the past thirty-five years "is owing to the great and simple operations of the Zollverein, (Customs Union), which is among the most important measures ever adopted in Europe." Frederick List, whose leading idea was to build up German industries by protection, had leading part in shaping that measure and said, in 1861, that "it affords protection from 20 to 60 per cent. on manufactures," and had "wrought a wonderful and excellent change." List was a student of Carey's great works, which are translated in German and Italian, and greatly prized by able Europeans. Australia and Canada, colonies of free trade England, have protective tariffs.

Sir Edward Sullivan, an eminent English writer opposed to their free trade system, says :

"Protection is as firmly drawn around all the native industries of Europe and America as it was twenty years ago, and generations will elapse before there is any sensible move in the opposite direction. If the English operative class are to wait till universal free trade overspreads the world, England must be turned into a Sleepy Hollow, to be awakened every hundred years, to see how foreigners are learning their duty to their neighbors as well as to themselves.

"We are told free trade principles are spreading ; why, in Prussia, Austria, Belgium, Switzerland, the idea even of opening their ports and markets, and inviting competition with their own industrial population, has never yet been mooted.

"France, Belgium, Switzerland, and Prussia have increased materially in wealth and prosperity during the last twenty years; capital has flowed steadily and with increasing rapidity into them; new manufactures have sprung up; existing industries have increased; trade has flourished; speculation and enterprise have taken the place of apathy and want of confidence. All this has taken place under a system of protection."

The Anglo-French Commercial treaty is sometimes called a free trade measure, but the Bradford Chamber of Commerce (English) complains that the French tariff is "unreasonable" and "excessive."

Sweden has its protective policy, as has every other European nation of any consequence.

The question of an inquiry into the operation of the commercial treaties being before the *Corps Legislatif,*

M. Louis Adolphe Thiers, afterward President of the French Republic, on the 22d of January, 1870, addressed it as follows :

"Every nation has three great affairs, which should be the object of its ardent and constant solicitude : liberty first, its greatness next, and finally its material prosperity. Liberty, which consists not merely in the right of the nation to criticise its government, but in the right of governing itself by its own hands, and conformably to its own ideas; greatness, which does not consist in subjecting its neighbors by brute force, but in exercising over them so much influence that no question shall be resolved in the world against its interests and security; prosperity, finally, which consists in drawing from its own soil, and from the genius of its inhabitants, the greatest possible amount of well-being.

"And do not think that this anxiety for the prosperity of the country has anything in common with that passion for material interests which the highest minds despise. There is no work of higher morality than to diminish the sum of the evils which weigh upon man, even in the most civilized societies. To make man less unhappy,—that is, to make him better,—it is to make him more just towards his government, to his fellow-beings, towards Providence itself.

"We are told that we would have a hot-house industry. What, then, are the nations which have sought to develop among themselves a national labor? They are the nations which are intelligent and free. When the foreigner brings them a product, after they have found it serviceable, they desire to imitate it. The nations which do not have this desire are the indolent nations of the East; intelligent and free nations seek to appropriate for themselves the products brought to them by foreign nations.

"It is urged that all the protections accorded to industry constitute monopolies, and that, to enrich a few monopolists, we burden the whole country. It is true there is a monopoly; but it is not in France, it is abroad. I desire to say that this little monopoly, which you accord to French industry, destroys the monopoly of foreign industry.

"When the linen industry was destroyed in France by the English production by power, a kilogram of thread was worth seven francs. We protected the linen industry in France. This protection permitted competition; and the French product compelled the English manufacturers to lower their prices to three francs fifty centimes.

"If England were the only country to produce certain objects, could you have them at the same price? Certainly not. It is competition, sustained by a just protection, which destroys foreign monopoly.

"Cotton is the grand textile of modern times. What is the importance of the industry of cotton among us ? We work up 600,000 or 700,000 bales, which represent in value 300,000,000 francs. When the cotton has been spun, woven, converted into plain cloths, printed cloths, haberdashery, hosiery, its value is forty times that sum. No industry has superior or equal importance. It is exposed to a double rivalry, that of the English and of the Swiss.

"The English have over us immense advantages : great capital, raw material, an enormous commerce, machines in the greatest number, coal at the cheapest price, and finally, which is a capital point, have the cheapness which results from an immense production. Whilst we move 6,000,000 of spindles, they move 34,000,000; we work up 600,000 bales of cotton, they work up 3,000,000.

"A kilogram of cotton yarn was worth twenty-seven francs in our war days; after peace it was as high as fourteen francs. We created a competition with England and it fell to three francs. Every time you protect a national product you cause the price of the domestic product to fall, and you prevent monopoly."

Turkey, ill-governed and ignorant, did not adopt a protective policy. Formerly she produced wool, silk, corn, and cotton, in large quantities; coal, iron and copper abound. Two hundred years ago her trade with Europe was large, and her merchants rich. But, in an evil hour, the government made a treaty with England and France, agreeing to charge no more than *three per cent.* duty on their imports, and to exempt their vessels from port charges. Great Britain forbade the exportation of her machinery to Turkey, as well as of her mechanics, who might have gone there to make it.

Of course, Turkish manufactures were ruined.

In Scutari, there were six hundred looms in 1812; but forty remained in 1821; and of two thousand weaving shops in Tournova in 1812, but two hundred were left in 1830. As in most purely agricultural countries, the cultivators are in debt. Twenty years ago the total exports of Turkey were but $33,000,000, while those of England to that country were but $11,000,000 yearly. Egypt, under the relentless grasp of British policy, is compelled to free trade, and is poor as well as powerless.

This summary of the protective policy of leading nations on the European continent refutes all contrary assertions.

CHAPTER V.
BRITISH FREE TRADE A DELUSION.

Forty years ago England adopted what she calls free trade, but what is really an inconsistent and deceptive approach toward a theory which no civilized nation ever carried out in practice. For centuries she was rigidly protective, and then modified her course; acting in both cases for what was held as her own best interest.

Brief paragraphs from an excellent address by H. H. Adams, of Cleveland, (Report of the Tariff Convention at Chicago, November, 1881,) will give glimpses of the rigidity of English protection and prohibition in past days:

"We find as far back in her history as 870 she enacted laws regulating the importation of goods manufactured on the continent by the Germans, and 'dues' were paid on goods. Even then they 'were not to forestall the market to the prejudice of the citizens.'

"In or about 1431, the laws prohibiting the importation of goods, except in English ships, were enacted. In 1504 an act of Parliament was made to regulate or restrict the importations of foreign-made silk (19 Henry, VII., c 21), prohibiting 'all persons for the future from bringing into the realm to be sold any manner of silk wrought by itself, or with any other stuff in any place out of this realm.'

"In 1567 a law was enacted that for the exportation of sheep the offender *should forfeit all his effects, suffer imprisonment for a year, and then have his left hand cut off in a market town, and on a market day, to be there nailed up; and for the second offense should suffer death.*'

"Some of the enactments of parliament for the years 1559 to 1603 were as follows:

The exportation of wool prohibited.
The coasting trade restricted to English vessels.
The importation of minerals, finished leather, etc., prohibited.
The immigration of skilled labor—smiths, miners, etc.—was encouraged, and duties laid on imported cloths

"In 1700 the importation of calicos, chintzes and muslins prohibited

"In 1720, any person found wearing a printed calico dress was fined five pounds, and the seller fined twenty pounds. The exportation of machinery for working flax was not repealed until England opened her ports to free trade in 1842.

"In 1646, after noting in preamble the benefits arising from customs, received on imports, from the plantations in Virginia and other places in America, Parliament inaugurated restrictive measures on goods exported from her colonies. 'None, in any of the ports of the said plantations, do suffer any ship or vessel to load any goods, of the growth of the plantations, and carry them to foreign ports, except in English bottoms.'

"We have to thank our good mother for her jealous care over us displayed by the act of Parliament (in 1731) prohibiting, under forfeiture of ship and cargo, carrying into any part of her American colonies, sugar, rum or molasses grown in the plantations of any foreign power."

In Oliver Cromwell's day that great man saw Holland gaining a large share of the ocean carrying trade of the world, her ships on every sea and her war vessels numerous and powerful. He felt that England must win this supremacy in peace and in war, and that a great commercial marine was the nursery of a powerful war navy. Under his inspiring guidance rigid navigation laws— forbidding the importation of foreign products save in English vessels, or in those of the country from whence those products came—were passed. This and other measures to encourage ship building crippled the carrying trade of Holland and built up a great English commercial marine and war navy. This policy was kept up so long as it seemed necessary and then came a change. Free ships were glorified, and navigation laws put aside, because England thought her fleets could sweep every sea fearless of competition, and be the carriers of every land.

Notwithstanding the free ship cry, the British government pays about $4,000,000 yearly to her ocean steamers for foreign postal service.

Vast accumulations of wealth, and improvements in mechanism and manufacturing processes with consequent low prices, had taken place in these centuries of protection, and a time came when the praises of free trade were sounded through the land and heard around the world. No doubt some of its advocates were wholly earnest and sincere in their ideas of its philanthropic benefits, and wished it carried out in good faith and honest consistency; but their ideals were not attained, and from the start inconsistency and grasping self-interest bore large sway.

MONOPOLY OF ALL MARKETS.

In the House of Lords, in one of the early debates on the question, Lord Goderich said:

"Other nations knew, as well as the noble lord opposite, and those who acted with him, that *what we* (the English) *meant by free trade, was nothing more nor less than, by means of the great advantages we enjoyed, to get the monopoly of all their markets for our manufactures, and to prevent them, one and all, from ever becoming manufacturing nations.*

"The policy that France acted on was that of encouraging its native manufactures, and it was a wise policy; because, if it were freely to admit our manufactures, it would speedily be reduced to an agricultural nation, and therefore a poor nation, as all must be that depend exclusively on agriculture."

So we learn from this precious revelation, that "British free trade" really means the monopoly of all markets, and the breaking down of all manufactures except their own. This English nobleman has at least the merit of frankness; but philanthropy is not apparent.

UNDERSELL, YET SEEM MAGNANIMOUS.

Only in 1840 commenced any change of note in British policy. A committee was then chosen, with Joseph Hume as chairman, "to inquire into the several duties levied on imports." What his aim would be may be judged from his wish, expressed in Parliament years before, that "the manufactures of the Continent might be strangled in their cradle." This committee's report said, that "the tariff presents neither congruity nor unity of purpose; no general principles seem to have been applied."

In 1842 the famed tariff of Sir Robert Peel was enacted. Was it free trade? Let Mr. Gladstone, Chancellor of the English Exchequer, answer: "It was an attempt to make a general approach to the following rules: *First*, the removal of prohibitions; *secondly*, the reduction of duties on manufactured articles and protective duties generally, to an average of twenty per cent. *ad valorem; thirdly*, on partially manufactured articles to rates not exceeding ten per cent.; *fourthly*, on raw materials to rates not over five per cent."

Simply a reducing to order of a chaos of centuries of patchwork acts, a reduction of some duties in view of the well known fact, that, with such reduction, their well established manufacturers would still undersell the world, and yet seem magnanimous, and low duties on food and raw materials, and articles partly manufactured, which, of course, would help home manufactures.

But Peel himself said, in his speech closing the debate on the bill: "I do not abolish all protective duties; on the contrary, the amended tariff maintains many duties that are purely protective, as distinguished from revenue duties."

The tariffs of 1845 and 1846 were similar in their general tenor, but of less consequence; carefully protective, *where necessary*, reduced where no home interest was hurt thereby, reduced indeed sometimes to benefit home interests, by giving raw material cheaper to the manufacturer.

In 1849 came, after warm and long debate, the virtual repeal of the corn laws, placing the duty on grain at a shilling a quarter, which was abolished in 1869.

It must be borne in mind that corn, in English commercial language, includes grain of all kinds, and that wheat was the grain most largely imported, so that the repeal of the duty on corn gave wheat, which was especially wanted for food for the people, free entrance to the ports of Great Britain. This repeal took place at the time when it was manifest that England could not feed her own people, and the free admission of foreign grains, and other farm products, would give them cheaper food. It was a necessity to reduce the price of breadstuffs at home, to stop English manufacturers from emigrating to the European Continent and starting their business abroad where food was cheaper. The repeal of the corn laws was an important step in the interest of British manufacturers, while the fact that a benefit to the working classes (which has not been realized) was confidently expected from it, enlisted a powerful and genuine philanthropic feeling in its favor, and cast a deceptive glamour of philanthropy around the whole free trade movement.

In 1874 the sugar duties were abolished, greatly to the injury, it was said, of the sugar refiners. It is now claimed that these were the last protection duties, and that Great Britain has "a free trade tariff, with duties for revenue only." The duty on corn was repealed because it was expected England could thus *buy* cheaper food; the duties on manufactured goods were repealed because England expected to *sell* cheaper than any other country.

THIS "FREE TRADE TARIFF" A FALSE CLAIM.

Plain facts will show the falsehood of that claim. Let us see it, however, as made by Mongredien, an English writer selected, not for his special ability but because the Cobden Club endorse him. In a small book published in New York, "History of the Free Trade Movement in England," he asks (see page 172):

"Is our present tariff one from which every shred and vestige of protection have been discarded? Is it truly and thoroughly a free trade tariff? That these questions must be answered in the affirmative it is easy to prove in the most conclusive manner." He then says that their revenue of $100,000,000 from customs duties is adduced by protectionists to show that they are not really free trade; declares "That such an inference is totally erroneous will presently be made manifest beyond all question;" and makes it manifest as follows: "We now levy import duties on only fifteen articles. Subjoined is a list of them, and to each is appended the amount of duty levied on it during the financial year 1879. (The amounts are given in dollars for convenience).

ARTICLES IMPORTED, NOT PRODUCED IN ENGLAND.

Tobacco	$42,949,405
Tea	20,846,165
Coffee	1,060,010
Chicory	333,995
Chocolate and cocoa	223,855
Dried fruit	2,546,170
Wine	7,348,550
	$75,307,650
Imported articles produced in England:— Spirits, gold and silver plate, beer vinegar, playing cards, pickles, malt, spruce,	$26,734,720
Total duties	$102,042,370

"It will be seen that three-fourths of the total sum is levied on articles which we do not and cannot produce. It is clear, therefore, that this portion cannot by any possibility be said to afford the slightest protection to native industry." He then says that the duty on imported spirits, of over $25,000,000, is a countervailing duty to balance the excise, or internal revenue tax. By the above statement he makes the free trade tariff case "manifest beyond all question." The slight difficulty in his statement is, *it is not true.* Instead of "only fifteen articles," there are fifty-three articles on their official list on which duties are levied. (Hon. W. D. Kelley, M. C., in Congressional debate.) He puts tobacco, coffee, chocolate and cocoa in three lines, craftily leaving his readers to infer that a uniform duty is levied on these articles, *quite contrary to the fact.* On *unmanufactured* tobacco the duty is 75 cents per pound, or 84 cents if of less than ten per cent. moisture. On *manufactured* tobacco the duty is 96 cents and 110 cents for two kinds, and on snuff and cigars from 100 cents to 130 cents per pound.

On *raw* coffee the duty is fourteen shillings per hundred pounds; *if roast or ground,* seventeen shillings. Cocoa husks and shells pay half a cent a pound, *if manufactured four cents. Observe, in each item a careful discrimination, and less duties on the raw material. This is protection to the British manufacturer.* It is not a duty according to the value. The finest leaf tobacco pays less than the poorest manufactured worth less per pound. The choicest Mocha or Java coffee, if raw, pays less than the poorest ground or roasted article of less value. *It is a protection to home manufactures.* Tobacco is the most important, and of this the United States sends them the largest part of their consumption. The duty on leaf tobacco is twenty cents less than on the lowest grade manufactured, and fifty cents less than on higher grades. Our exports of leaf tobacco to Great Britain in 1880 were 33,996,486 pounds; average valuation $10\tfrac{9}{10}$ cents per pound; duty at least 75 cents or $25,497,364, at the modest rate of seven hundred per cent. or more. Of manufactured tobacco we sent them, the same year, less than one-fifth in value compared to the leaf ($720,554 to $3,693 799) and not one-tenth as much in weight probably.

That pretended "free trade tariff," on over forty per cent. of the total dutiable imports of Great Britain, so discriminates between manufactured and raw materials, by duties from twenty-five to forty-five per cent. higher on the first than on the last, as to give effective protection to her own manufactures. Meanwhile Mr. Mongredien and his like assert that "every shred or vestige of protection has been discarded from it!" Plate gold has a duty of $4.08 per ounce, and plate silver 36 cents per ounce; the bullion, or raw material being free. This "shred" the Cobden club man conveniently ignores.

This pretense of free trade appears all the more absurd when we see that the British government levies duties on the goods of other countries—tea, coffee, the tobacco of the United States, etc.—when brought into their ports, but asks that those countries shall levy no duties on her goods. Is this the boasted freedom of commercial intercourse?

John McGregor, one of the joint secretaries of the British Board of Trade, after a laborious and searching inquiry into the industrial affairs of almost every European country, came to the conclusion:

"That England, with all her natural advantages of position, *which no other country possesses in the same degree,* and the intelligence and industry of her artisans, together with capital, machinery, and other elements, such as coal and iron, and the superiority of her harbors for exportation, and many other internal advantages as to carriage and intercourse, should have nothing but fiscal taxation—that is, *duties for revenue only ;* have *no protection at all,* but only equalize upon equitable principles the system of taxing the population for revenue; *and they may then meet the people of all other nations with their manufactures, in every country in the world, and in most articles undersell them.*"

An emphatic suggestion of Mr. McGregor's gives the key to the English policy—professed "duties for revenue only * * no protection at all." The cry in this country for a "tariff for revenue only" is the echo of this British voice.

While it is important to show the character and results of English legislation on this subject, and the motives for their active interest in our affairs, we must bear in mind that even if free trade works well there, that is no reason why we should adopt it. The policy of each country must be shaped by its own condition. Yet if, in a country the best prepared for free trade of any in the world, that policy works badly, its poor results surely add weight against our adopting it.

REACTION AGAINST FREE TRADE IN ENGLAND.

While free trade is the policy of the English majority there is not the unanimity in its favor, either among the working classes or the leaders in thought, that we are led to suppose. A strong reaction against it has sprung up of late, its opponents asking for "fair trade" and "reciprocity" but really accepting the protective idea. An able work by Sir Edward Sullivan, "Protection to Native Industry," has passed through several editions in that country and has been republished here. Some extracts will show the method and weight of his arguments. He says the movement started among the workingmen, and then goes on as follows:

"Is it not absurd, and stupid, and irritating to the working classes to admit duty free all they produce, to tax all they consume; to admit duty free clocks, watches, silk, paper, gloves, glass, ribbons, hats, boots, shoes, millinery, the finer kind of cotton goods, and linen, and scores of other industries and to continue a heavy tax on cocoa, coffee, sugar, tea and tobacco?

"The operative class are the largest consumers of cocoa, tea, coffee, sugar and tobacco; and they are the actual producers of all the articles of foreign manufacture that are admitted duty free into our markets.

"The present state of affairs hits them doubly hard, they suffer both ways; the value of their wages is diminished by the amount of the customs duty charged on the necessary articles of food they consume; and the amount of their wages is reduced by the free admission of foreign articles of manufacture to compete with those they produce.

"At present emigration is confined to the operative class; but there is another emigration that is threatened that will be far more ruinous in its effects, viz.: an emigration of capital and manufacturers; what can the British operative do if his employer and capital disappear together? * * * * * *

"There cannot exist the least doubt that our manufacturing position is on the wane."

* * * * * * * * *

(Complaints also come from England of distress in the agricultural interests.)

"Free traders renounce all logic and facts when discussing their favorite dogma: they are, indeed, the most disingenuous of arguers. I declare, that, as constantly as I have heard the subject discussed, I never once heard a free trader have the honesty to attribute the increased trade of the world in general, and of England as part of it, to its true causes, viz., the vast increase in the circulating medium and the general application of steam, but always to what they choose to call free trade. To ignore these illimitable agencies, and to ascribe all progress to the pigmy efforts of a small school of political economists in England, is to reverse the old proverb, and to imagine the mouse bringing forth the mountain.

"The increased foreign commerce of England, during the last twenty years, is attributed to her free trade policy; and we are led, by implication, to understand that she is the only nation that has advanced in commercial activity during that period.

"Free traders point with triumph to our board of trade returns of exports and imports, and exclaim triumphantly, This is our doing; but they ignore the fact—it cannot be through ignorance—that the board of trade returns in France, Switzerland, Prussia, Belgium, and Austria, show results far more satisfactory, a proportionate increase of trade far exceeding our own.

"Take France, for instance, as being our nearest neighbor, and compare her wealth and commercial position now with what it was twenty years ago, and it will at once be granted that, however great may be the blessings of free trade, sound progress is not incompatible with the strictest protection. The bullion in the Bank of France is now, in 1869, forty-seven millions,—twenty-seven millions higher than it was in 1844, and sixteen millions higher than in 1853: the bullion in the Bank of England is seventeen millions,—two millions higher than in 1844, three millions less than in 1853!

"In France, in 1868, the exports and imports balanced within twenty millions. In England, the excess of imports was over sixty millions! and in 1869 it will, in all probability, reach one hundred millions."

In the Nineteenth Century (a leading London Magazine) of August, 1881, Sir Edward Sullivan has an article on "Isolated Free Trade," from which an extract shows the feeling against free trade of many English workmen:

"The organization of the working classes is very complete and very strong, and at this moment the whole of it is being concentrated on this point. Already a number of operatives, far more than is necessary to turn a general election, have, through their delegates, given in their adherence to the Fair Trade League.

"The workingmen are not working out the question by the abstract reasoning of others, but by their own experience; they know nothing of political economy, but they know what were the promises of the apostles of free trade, and they know what are the results. Bankers and brokers and dealers in stocks and importers of foreign manufactures may tell them that they are fools and do not know when they are well off. That may be so, but they know when they are badly off, and they are badly off now.

"The reports of their delegates state that a very large proportion of the operative population of Great Britain (they put it at one-third) is out of work; that the rest have not, on an average, more than four days' work a week; that for five or six years they have been consuming their savings and the funds of their trade societies. One rich trade society has paid no less than £200,000 in 'work pay' during the last five years, and reduced its capital to less than £100,000.

"Whatever the wealth of the country may be, it has not penetrated down to them. Every year this wealth is accumulating into fewer hands; every year the gulf between rich and poor becomes deeper and broader. It is calculated that there are at this moment 14,500,000 of the people with less than 10s. 6d. a week to live on. The operatives look abroad, and they see and hear from their mates what is the condition of national wealth in France and America, that there the fertilizing stream has descended to all classes, and they find the very reverse is the case: that wealth is daily becoming more generally distributed, that every year the gulf between rich and poor is getting narrower and shallower. They see and hear that the operatives in France and America have far steadier work, higher wages in proportion, and are increasing more rapidly in material prosperity than the work-people of Great Britain, and they are beginning to ask why. They know that they are, man for man, as good as their rivals; that in mechanical skill, in aptitude for hard work, in mineral wealth, in national capital, &c., they are their superiors. Why, then, are they not equally advancing in material prosperity?

"The stock arguments of the big loaf, the natural antagonism between producers and consumers, between employers and employed, &c., have been disproved by the rate and reality of the American progress.

"'I can hardly allow myself to believe,' said Lord Derby, 'that America will long maintain at the public expense a privileged class of manufacturers and producers.' But the American people laugh at this; they know that every prosperous manufacturer means a hundred or two of prosperous workmen, and every ruined manufacturer, one or two hundred ruined workmen; that if the employer is losing money the employed cannot be making it. More than this, they understand that manufacturing and agricultural industries are inseparably bound up together, that prosperous manufactures mean prosperous agriculture, and *vice versa;* that each consumes what the other produces; that each is the best customer to the other."

Other able English writers have sent out like pamphlets and books, largely read. "The Stagnation of Trade; Its Causes and Cure," by R. Burn, of Manchester;

"Free Trade a Gigantic Mistake," by James Roberts; "Sophisms of Free Trade," by Sir J. B. Boyle, are among these.*

Able articles have been published in newspapers, of which an extract from a letter to the Sheffield *Telegraph* by Mr. Wood, a manufacturer, may serve as a specimen:

"In 1868 the excess of our imports over exports reached the ruinous sum of £116,042,000 ($580,000,000) more by £13,000,000 than the whole export of textile manufactures. What must be the effect of free admission of 362,820 clocks and watches; 7,757,000 yards of cottons; 404,544 hundred weight of glass; 468,240 pairs of shoes; 10,714 pairs of gloves; 3,866,130 pounds of silks; 2,261,000 pounds of woolen and worsted yarns? What amount of labor would not these articles have found for our half-starved people? While certain articles, such as tea, coffee, sugar, etc., which we cannot produce, are admitted at *heavy duties*, other

---

*In a London pamphlet by A. McEwen, in 1879, it is stated that the British Board of Trade Reports make the excess of imports over exports for the four years, 1875-8, four hundred and eighty million pounds sterling, or $2,400,000,000. Mr. Mongredien counts merchants' and carriers' profits, and brings it down to $1,155,000,000; which McEwen accepts, but thinks too low. Hon. L. H. Dudley, late U. S. consul at Liverpool, makes the excess of British imports over exports for ten years, 1870-9, $4,164,618,761, and says the balance was against her every year. He gives the excess of United States exports over imports in the same ten years at $329,921,523. They bought immensely more than they sold, while we sold more than we bought. In the long run the tide sets against free trade England.

A favorite mode of some English writers to show the alleged prosperity which free trade has brought their country is to give statistics of their trade, *and leave out comparisons with that of other countries*. Mongredieu, for instance, says: "In 1840 the foreign trade of the United Kingdom (exports and imports combined) was £172,133,000; in 1878 it amounted to £614,255,000, a marvelous rate of increase."

The foreign trade of the United States in 1840 was $202,846,941; in 1878 it reached $1,153,809,261. That is, the British trade increased 350 per cent., but the American trade over 500 per cent. If the first was a "marvelous increase" under free trade, the last was a much more marvelous increase under protection through most of the time, and far the larger part of that increase from 1864 to 1878, our period of permanent protection.

The trade of protective France increased in a greater ratio than that of England in the same period.

articles, which we can produce, and our countrymen are literally dying to produce, are admitted *free*, such as silks, woolens, watches, clocks, etc. *　*　*　*　*　*

"At this moment about one in every eighteen persons in England and Wales is in receipt of parochial relief. For pauperism in 1853 £4,929,000 was paid; in 1868 £7,500,000. Since 1853 upwards of 3,000,000 of our people have emigrated, *principally to extreme protective countries*, where their labor has found better reward."

There is a mournful pathos in the address of a meeting of iron-workers in South Staffordshire to their employers. They say:

"We ask you, gentlemen, can you expect that we will continue, 'like dumb, driven cattle,' to accept with indifference the present state of things as if we had become 'living dead men?' The low price of labor and the high price of living has driven and is driving your best workmen from the country, to compete with us in the labor markets of the world."

Proof of this distress comes from other sources. In an article in the London *Contemporary Review*, July, 1880, by an American, Mr. Herbert J. Leffingwell, he says: "Is it true, as the Earl of Carnvaron stated last winter in the House of Lords, that the amount of disasters and poverty is greater than has been known for a long time? Is it true, that, by the register general's reports, one person in every thirty-six in England and Wales is a pauper?" The London *Daily Telegraph*, in July, 1879, said: "Scores of destitute men and women, usually of advanced age, utterly homeless, die from cold and hunger in the streets of London every year."

In a speech in the United States Senate, in December, 1881, Hon. J. S. Morrill spoke of "five thousand houses now marked 'to let' in Sheffield, and ten thousand in Birmingham," and a decrease in the total of British exports and imports from 1873 to 1880 of $250,000,000 are painful proofs of decreased prosperity.

THE COBDEN CLUB.

Great Britain is poor in agricultural resources, with a narrow island territory, land in few hands and rented to tenants, a dense population which its farms cannot feed, and magnificent deer parks stretching for miles around the palaces of titled noblemen, while the poor pine in want in sight of their enchanting but jealously-guarded borders.

It is estimated that she must import food valued at $800,000,000 yearly, and raw materials (cotton, &c.,) to use in her manufactures valued at about $650,000,000, and export $1,200,000,000 worth of manufactures. Her very life depends on cheap food, cheap raw materials, and a wide command of the world's markets; and it is held of vital importance by her leading business men that free trade sentiments should spread over the world, that England may crush out competing foreign manufactures. To this end the Cobden Club was formed, bearing the name of a great Englishman identified with free trade, and greatly respected for certain noble qualities. This club has among its members two hundred members of Parliament, several Cabinet Ministers, and some sixty persons from the United States, or twice as many as from any other country.

It aims to enlist the power of rank, of education and ability, and of social and political influence.

Especial care is taken to have an array of members from this country. A leading object is to convert the United States to free trade, or at least to unsettle and damage our tariff, or keep up an agitation, and so check our manufactures. This is not strange in view of the magnitude of our trade and the pressure of British necessity for it. Our imports from Great Britain for ten years preceding 1876 were $1,813,000,000. To keep this immense trade is life, to decrease it is disaster, to lose it is death. Hence the sending of Cobden Club tracts by car-loads over the West and South, the visits of English members of Parliament to this country, and the formation of free trade leagues and clubs.

Lord Derby presided at the Cobden Club dinner in London, in July, 1881, and said in his speech, that "sooner or later free trade must become a *sectional* question in the United States." Doubtless this aristocratic nobleman would like to make it such, and hence his assertion.

The purpose and aim of certain classes in England is to break down our manufactures, or to check their progress, which is so necessary to supply the constantly increasing wants of our growing millions, and thus make room for the products of British factories. It is the same spirit and system by which they opened China to the vile opium trade, of which the British government had the monopoly, but the methods are different. We are too strong to be pushed into free trade at the bayonet point, and so a pamphlet war is carried on, and the army of invasion is made up of Cobden Club tracts and other like craft.

There is no European nation except the English that endeavors to interfere with the domestic affairs of this country. The breaking down of our system would be very much for the interest of the French, Germans, Swiss, Italians, and Russians, as well as for that of the English, but we hear of no plans in either of those countries for an offensive intermeddling with our affairs. Many Englishmen seem to be fully persuaded that the

Americans know nothing of political economy, and that they are utterly incompetent to manage their own affairs; and they do not hesitate to say so frankly.

At a recent Cobden Club meeting it was said that nearly a million free trade pamphlets had been sent to this country within a few years and largely used in our congressional campaigns. That club has also offered prizes of gold and silver medals for the best essays on political economy—free trade of course—by students in American colleges. Suppose a protective tariff club in New York should send their tracts to England and offer prizes to the Cambridge and Oxford university students for the best essays on protection. Our British cousins would say: "Mind your own business!"—and with good reason.

WE MUST PROTEST.

The bonds of a common race and language are to be borne in mind; the warm sympathy between us and the people of Great Britain on some important subjects to be kept alive; the great service done us in our days of trial by eminent Englishmen—some of them leading free traders—is to be held in fit honor; but we must be just to ourselves, and make strong protest against the unjust and selfish policy of British free trade.

A Parliament Commission, in 1854, in a report on the mining population, spoke of "immense losses which employers incur in bad times, in order to destroy foreign competition, and to gain and keep possession of foreign markets," of works being carried on for this purpose "at an aggregate loss of three or four hundred thousand pounds sterling," and of the ability of a few wealthy capitalists "to overwhelm all foreign competition," and thus "step in for the whole trade when prices revive."

As an illustration of this process—very costly to us and equally profitable to these British capitalists—let us look at the trade in railroad iron from 1840 to 1854. First, these men had spent money here largely to break down our tariff of 1842, and get instead the lower tariff of 1846, with its *ad valorem* rates, under which frauds in the importer's invoice could push duties down. Then in 1849 and 1850 more than 200,000 tons of railroad iron was pushed into the country at $40 per ton, and our mills at home closed up and their business ruined. This was the plot to "gain and keep the market," and the harvest was at hand. From 1850 to 1854 the British, controlling the market and running up the price, sold us 800,000 tons of railroad iron at $75 per ton.

With an adequate protection, our own mills could have furnished the iron at $50 per ton; but for want of it they were stopped, and thus $60,000,000 went into the hands of British capitalists, and soon came, inevitably, the terrible distress of the crisis of 1857.

It is easy to find, this side of the Atlantic, interested parties, and honest free traders sincerely devoted to a delusion, to co-operate with the Cobden Club.

ENGLISH CONTRIBUTORS TO FREE TRADE FUNDS IN NEW YORK.

In May, 1869, the American Free Trade League in New York raised $42,000, and published a list of contributors. Among these were A. B. Sands & Co., drug importers, relatives of Baring Brothers, London bankers, $6,257; H. Marshall, agent Black Ball Line Liverpool Packets, and foreign bankers, $5,500; Grinnell,

British Free Trade a Delusion. 43

Minturn & Co., ship owners, Minturn brother-in-law to Baring, $3,800; Mr. Pell, of Liverpool and London Globe Insurance Co., $842; Naylor & Co., English steel house, $500; Mall & Co., importers, Mall Belgian Consul, $500; and so on up to $30,000 pledged by such men. The reason why these gentlemen of foreign lineage or connections are so especially solicitous and liberal in this matter is not far to seek. *The London Mining Journal* says: "If this League succeeds, *we may hope for a very large trade from that country.*" This solves the mystery. It must be borne in mind that New York is the centre from whence goes out aid and comfort to free trade efforts all over the land. Were it not for such help, there would be little agitation. It is not spontaneous, does not spring up among the people, but is fanned into forced life by aid of interested parties *largely English.* The *Philadelphia Press* says that the *New York Journal of Commerce* (free trade) admitted that "nine-tenths of the money pledged to the New York Free Trade League comes from foreigners."

EARLY ENGLISH FEAR OF OUR MANUFACTURES.

English solicitude touching our manufactures is of early date. In 1817 the House of Commons declared, "that the erecting manufactories in the colonies tended to lessen their dependence upon Great Britain." The Board of Trade and Plantations, in 1731–32, in pursuance of an order of the House of Commons to inquire into the industrial affairs of the plantations, charged that in New England, New York, Pennsylvania, and Maryland,—"in the colonies northward of Virginia,"—the colonies "had fallen into the manufacture" of woolen and linen cloth; that they raised flax and hemp, which they manufactured into "a coarse sort of cloth, bags, traces, and halters," to supply the domestic demand; that they had established woolen mills for domestic manufactures, and that linen and cotton, for shirting, were made; that they "manufactured brown hollands for women's wear," and that the Assembly of Massachusetts had voted a bounty of thirty shillings for every piece of duck or canvas manufactured in the province; that great quantities of hats and leather were manufactured and exported to Spain, Portugal, and the West Indies; that in Massachusetts they had set up a paper-mill; that they had established iron works, six furnaces and nineteen forges, and one slitting mill, for the manufacture of bar iron, and of "cast iron, or hollow ware,"—all sorts of iron for ships,"—and "a manufactory for nails;" and that they "built many brigantines and small sloops," which they sold in the West Indies.

All this was very bad in the opinion of the British Parliament, and they passed severe preventive laws.

The exportation from England of artisans or tools for making woolens, silk, or iron, was prohibited. Lord Cobham said the colonists should not even make a horse-nail. In 1750 pig iron from this country was admitted *free* into British ports, to be worked into finer forms there, but the erection or "continuance" of any iron mill here forbidden under penalty of from £200 to £500. One great grievance of our forefathers in those colonial days was the persistent resolve of the mother country to crush our manufactures, and so keep us poor and dependent; and to escape from this was a leading motive for declaring our national independence.

HANDS OFF!

We may wish Great Britain such success as the skill and persistent vigor of her people are entitled to; such share of the world's work and trade as she can fairly win; but when she seeks to paralyze our enterprise, cripple our industry, and degrade our civilization by propagating in our midst the delusions of British free trade,. we must cry out: Hands off!

One significant fact should be borne in mind. *The policy urged by American free traders has the full sympathy and support of British traders and manufacturers, because it is for their benefit.*

This intermeddling, this profuse advice thrust on us uncalled for, as though we were incompetent and foolish, this greed of gain under the guise of philanthropic wish for our good, we must repel and repudiate.

Of such intermeddling the *Chicago Western Manufacturer*, of October 18, 1881, gives proofs. It tells how one Professor Sheldon from London called at the office of "one of the leading agricultural journals in that city" and urged its editor to publish " entire or in abstract in his columns" the Mongredien Western Farmer pamphlet, especially that portion of it urging those farmers " to give their support to no candidate for Congress who does not pledge himself, if elected, to propose or vote for the abolition of import duties." To his honor the editor decidedly declined this cool proposal.

The *Manufacturer* also says :

"Another agent and correspondent of the Cobden Club, duly delegated, one Professor Bigelow of New York, was in this city a day or two recently, consulting with local free traders. He was going to Indiana, well supplied with British pamphlets, with which he proposed to influence votes against candidates for Congress who were not pledged to propose or vote for the abolition of import duties, if elected."

Suppose American protective tariff agents in England meddling with an election and spreading documents. All England would ring with denunciations of Yankee interference, and the poor agents would beat a hasty retreat.

The people of this country are led by these things to suspect that whenever a free trade crusade starts here, no matter how carefully hidden the wires may be, *an Englishman stands at the other end of the line.*

CHAPTER VI.

THE FREE TRADE FALSEHOOD, THAT A PROTECTIVE TARIFF IS A TAX ON THE CONSUMER, REFUTED.

It is a constant and emphatic assertion of free traders that a protective tariff taxes the consumer. They assume that the duty on an imported article is added to its price, at the cost of the buyer, and added also to the price of like articles made here. If, for instance, we import 50,000 yards of a certain kind of woolen cloth, with a duty of fifty cents per yard, and make 200,000 yards of the same kind at home, that duty is added to the price of both the imported and domestic goods, and the buyers pay $75,000 extra; of which government gets $25,000, and $50,000 goes to the protected home manufacturers, who thus craftily enrich themselves, while professing to benefit the people they rob. This is held up as the alleged effect and lasting result of what Professor Perry calls "our iniquitous and accursed tariff."

This assertion is a gross assumption, without proof and contrary to fact, and is upheld as the strong hold of the free trade argument. Doubtless there are those who honestly hold it true, but it is false in origin and deceptive in aim.

On the contrary, facts in this chapter will prove this statement: *No protective duty was ever levied on a single article, the home manufacture of which grew to large proportions under that duty, without the price to the consumer growing cheaper,—the duty thus being a boon instead of a tax.*

To treat a tariff as a tax is a shrewd, yet shallow device. George Basil Dixwell, of Boston, reviewing Professor Sumner on "Protective Taxes," says:

"A tax is not necessarily a burthen. If the money be well spent, and give us good roads, water works, police, and good government, at what they ought to cost, then a tax is a great blessing; but, unfortunately, the money is often spent recklessly and foolishly, and so, *through abuse,* the very name of tax becomes offensive. The free trader avails himself of this existing prejudice, with the effect of disgusting the reader with protection at the outset, in advance of all argument. The word tax also gives two false impressions: first, that all protected articles cost the consumer more than they would if not protected; and second, that when they cost more, the consumer gets no counterbalancing or greatly overbalancing advantages."

With brief preliminaries, let us "to the law and the testimony," for this case is to be settled by facts, not by assertions. In a free trade meeting in this city the speaker said, with an air of confident assurance· "Of course the duty is added to the prices, for the importer pays it, adds it to the cost of his goods, and then sells them as cheap as makers here sell theirs." To tell half the truth and ignore the rest is a sharp lawyer's way to win his case, but is *not* a full or fair statement. He ignored the fact that our competition compels the foreign maker and the importer to reduce their prices, and that *we reap the benefit,*—a benefit impossible without such competition by our home industries, built up under protection.

Let up put an English statement in contrast with this free trade assertion. Robert P. Porter, a member of the tariff commission, now a correspondent of the *New York Tribune*, from England, especially describing the industrial condition of Great Britain, in a letter from Bradford, the center of the great worsted industry, says:

"If I were asked what the keen practical Bradford manufacturer thought on economic questions, I should frankly reply that after an experience of a generation some of them are prepared to prove that *tariff duties come more largely out of the producer than the consumer*. Some of them demonstrated this quite conclusively to me. One of the most prominent said:

"'The truth is, the higher the foreign tariff the lower we must make our goods and the less we can afford to pay labor. The least possible reduction in the United States tariff will be a grand thing for Bradford, but how it will affect your industries I can hardly say. We are obliged to sell our goods in France for the same price as we did before they enacted their higher tariff, and the Bradford manufacturer is paying that duty, not the French consumers of the goods. I know from practical experience what I am talking about.'"

In a speech in Cooper Institute, Feb. 1, 1883, Dexter A. Hawkins, an eminent New York lawyer, said:

"Some years ago I attended by invitation the monthly meeting of the Hardware Trade at Sheffield, England.

"Their exports then were chiefly to this country.

"An eminent manufacturer, in addressing the meeting, inveighed with great bitterness against the American tariff. He said he had examined the question with great care, and such examination demonstrated that the English manufacturer was paying at least one-half of the tariff on all the goods he exported to America; and they must break down our tariff, at whatever cost, or it would build up American rivals to the extent, at least, of supplying entirely our home market, and then England would have to pay the whole tariff or lose the market; and when that point was reached, she would have to compete with the American manufacturer in every foreign market, then her own almost exclusively.

"Another English manufacturer a few years ago, while lobbying at Washington against our tariff, confessed to a free trade congressman that the protective tariff duties, in the long run, came almost wholly out of the foreign producer ; that if they only came out of the domestic consumer the foreign manufacturer would not care a button about our tariff laws."

Such testimonies outweigh the special plea, the aim of which was to make a fragment of the case appear as the whole. A half truth is more deceptive than a bare falsehood.

The grave Senator in Washington declares with ponderous solemnity : "A tariff is a tax, added to the price of all articles on which it is levied, and it compels the people to pay the same added cost on all like home made articles." The shallow politician at the corner grocery, the boy in the debate at the country school house, and the college professor in his rhetorical treatise make the same assertion. School-boy and professor and senator are on the same level. They remind one of Mark Twain's reply to an invitation to lecture before an agricultural society. As he tells the story he wrote them : "Gentlemen, I am happy to accept your invitation. I think myself especially qualified, for I know nothing about agriculture."

Augustus Mongredien, in his British tract, "The Western Farmer of America," (a poor affair, lifted into brief importance by being sent over here and widely distributed from the Cobden Club in London,) rolls this statement "like a sweet morsel under his tongue."

With a complacency only equalled by the effrontery of the assertion, he says that "our tariff makes the overcharge our western farmers have to pay for all the manufactured goods they consume $400,000,000 yearly," which these hard working people "needlessly and heedlessly throw away." "The average duty on imports is the measure of the difference between the prices they pay and what they would pay were foreign articles admitted free." This is the Cobden Club voice, echoed by Senator and schoolboy alike. From this comes his conclusion that a duty for revenue only, raised on articles we do not produce, may be a necessity, but that a tariff for protection and revenue, raised on articles we import and also make or produce, is a fraud and a robbery of the people. This is assumption, based on assertions which facts repudiate, and which the laws of trade make absurd.

ALEXANDER HAMILTON.

The philosophy of the whole matter was well given by that great statesman, Alexander Hamilton, in his famous report in 1791, as secretary of the treasury:

"But, though it were true that the immediate and certain effect of a tariff was an increase of price, it is universally true that the contrary is the ultimate effect with every successful manufacture. When a domestic manufacture has attained to perfection, and has engaged in the prosecution of it a competent number of persons, it can be afforded, and accordingly seldom or never fails to be sold cheaper, in process of time, than the foreign article for which it is a substitute. The internal competition which takes place soon does away with everything like monopoly, and by degrees reduces the price of the article to the minimum of a reasonable profit on the capital employed. This accords with the reason of the thing and with experience."

This eminent man had not learned that a tariff is a tax on the consumer! Washington, Jefferson, Jackson, Webster, and other great men were in equal ignorance, and so advocated tariffs for protection. That friend of the people, Abraham Lincoln, declared himself an advocate of a protective tariff. Professor Reuleaux, president of the German Commission at our Centennial Exposition, went home and said: "The present condition of American manufactures shows the fallacy of the free trade doctrine that the productions of a country are raised in price by protective duties."

Even if a duty sometimes keeps prices up for a brief time compensations come at once, and lower prices soon follow. Free traders craftily ignore the compensations that they may the more plausibly deny the benefits. Take, for instance, the Brinkerhoff charge that $40,000,-000 went into the pockets of our iron makers in 1868, as a result of the "iniquitous tax" imposed on the people by the duty on iron, and grant (what is not true) that the price was raised that amount. Mr. A. S. Hewitt, in his report as United States commissioner, said: "The entire difference in the cost of making iron here and in England is the wages," which he gave as 87 cents to $1.00 per day there and $2.00 here. So we find that the Brinkerhoff $40,000,000 went to the workmen, and the farmers got about $10,000,000 of it.

Napoleon created the best sugar industry in France under a prohibitive embargo. Sugar was high, but it soon fell, and hundreds of thousands of tons of beet sugar are made in France to-day, practically their entire consumption, and it is exported to the London market.

History tells the same story in different countries,— the building up of vast industries, and the cheapening of prices under protective tariffs. In England woolens formerly had a high tariff, sometimes a prohibition, and the duty on iron was raised a score of times, from $2.50 up to $35 per ton, *and woolens and iron grew cheaper all the time.* If tariff is a tax, they should have gone up higher than a kite!

It should be borne in mind that the sole aim of cheapness tends to inferiority in quality. The excellence and taste of French goods sell them everywhere. We have reached a like excellence in some manufactures, and it should be aimed at in all, for the best goods find the best markets. "Cheap and nasty" is the expressive phrase applied to some British products. The *London Times* says:

"The Americans succeed in supplanting us by novelty of construction and excellency of work. They do not attempt to undersell us in the mere matter of price. Our goods may still be the cheapest, but they are no longer the best; and in the country where an axe, for instance, is an indispensable instrument, the best article is the cheapest, whatever it may cost. Settlers and emigrants soon find this out, and they have found it out to the prejudice of Birmingham trade.

Our American silk goods rival foreign silks in excellence, and begin to surpass them in genuineness—more silk and less dye stuffs.

But have prices in the United States gone up with protective tariffs, or was Hamilton right in saying that the domestic manufacture "seldom or never fails to be sold cheaper in process of time than the foreign article. * * * The internal competition soon does away with monopoly?"

COTTON MANUFACTURES.

In 1860 our cotton manufactures reached $116,000,000 in value. In 1880, with twenty years of stable protection, their value was $192,773,960, employing 175,187 operatives, and paying $42,000,000 wages, at rates forty per cent. higher (see *Commercial Bulletin*) than in 1860.

The New York Secretary of the Free Trade League asserted, without proof, in Chicago, a few years ago, that spool-cotton was "taxed 52 per cent.," the consumers paying the tax. A reliable correspondent of the

Hartford (Ct.) *Post*, in 1869, made the following statement in reply,—his simple facts demolishing the assertion. That the case stands now about as then, is proved by the export of our spool cotton to foreign markets, where its superior quality is prized. The *Post* writer said:

"The average importation of spool-cotton into New York for three consecutive years ending June 30, 1861, was 6,685,200 dozen per annum, and under a duty of 24 per cent. *ad valorem*, yielded a revenue to the government of $365,063.04 per annum.

"The importation of spool-cotton into New York in 1868 was 3,519,573 dozen; duties on the same, $822,276.98.

"We have no data to show the importations of this article into other ports in the country, but will suppose it to be 500,000, or the whole importation of the year to be 4,000,000 dozen; amount of American six-cord thread manufactured in 1868, 2,000,000 dozen; amount of American enameled thread manufactured, 8,000,000 dozen.

"It appears that not less than 14,000,000 dozen spool-cotton will be consumed in this country the present year, more than two-thirds of which is of American manufacture.

"Up to a late period the foreign manufacturers controlled the price of thread in our market; at present the American manufacturers control the price.

"For two or three years foreign thread remained steady at $1.10 to $1.15 per dozen; it is now selling at 80 to 90 cents per dozen, a decline in price of 30 cents per dozen in two years, a saving to the consumers of foreign thread of $1,200,000 the present year, while the decline in the price of American spool-cotton, owing to strong competition, has been reduced more than 50 per cent., a still further saving of $2,000,000. The following is a summary of the results of a high duty on spool-cotton. The revenue to the government has been more than doubled; the American manufacture of thread has been largely increased, while the price of labor in these thread mills is still as high as during the war, and the consumers of thread are saving $3,000,000 per annum through the strong competition which has sprung up between the American and foreign manufacturers."

COTTON PIECE GOODS.

Cottons, imported at fifty cents a yard before our mills were built, have been exported at six cents under a high tariff, and of a better quality. The shrewd Chinamen say we use more cotton and less starch than the English in the cloth sent to them. Cotton hosiery was reduced in price nearly one-half from 1860 to 1868. Delaines, formerly imported at thirty-five cents to fifty cents, were made here in 1868 at twenty cents of equal quality.

Our brown, bleached, printed and dyed cottons compete with the English in foreign lands, and the prices are *lower* under a *higher* tariff, as the following table shows: *

Articles.	1860.	1882.
Standard sheetings, per yard	8.73 cents	8.00 cents
Standard drillings, "	8.92 "	8.00 "
Bleached shirtings, "	15.50 "	12.35 "
Printed calicoes, "	9.50 "	6.17 "
Printing cloths, "	5.44 "	4.00 "

In view of the fact that some kinds of cotton goods are as low in the United States as anywhere in the world, how foolish the assertion that the normal price of an article is its American price minus the duty! The tariff on standard sheetings is 57 per cent.; this percentage from 8.00 cents (the price above quoted), is 4.50 cents, leaving the alleged foreign price 3.40 cents per yard, or less than half what it is. The tariff on standard cotton is no more a burthen or tax on the home consumer than that on wheat or beef. It is simply a barrier against our market being flooded by English goods sent at less than

---

* This table, and that on woolens, are from the *Boston Commercial Bulletin.*

cost—their favorite game "to break down competition and step in for the whole market when prices revive."

This cry against a tariff as a monstrous tax on consumers was the staple of free trade speeches in 1842; and Henry Clay, in his Raleigh speech in 1844, told how a Western farmer "pricked the bubble *theory* with the needle *fact.*" The demagogue on the stump cried out to him: "Do you know, my friend, that these tariff monopolists make you pay six cents a yard (the duty) more than you ought for the shirt on your back?" The farmer replied: "I suppose it must be so, but I can't quite see how, for I only paid five and a half cents a yard for it."

In this matter of cotton goods it should be known that the raw cotton in 1876–81 was two to three cents a pound higher than in 1855–60, and wages were higher. Here we have the raw material higher, the duty higher, wages higher, *and the goods lower.*

SILKS.

By the census it appears that we made $16,262,157 worth of silks of all kinds in 1874, and $34,410,463 worth in 1880; paying $9,146,705 in wages, at from $3.37 to $24.71 per week.

W. C. Wykoff, U. S. Census Agent, writes as follows: "It may be stated with certainty that the average decline in value of silk goods is not less than 25 per cent., and probably over 30 per cent., in fifteen years. * * * Machine twist (sewing silk on spools for use on sewing machines) is better than the French or Italian. It is the oldest branch of our silk industry. For years its manufacturers have been engaged in the severest competition, both as to cheapness and superior quality.

It is greatly improved, but the price is a third less." Here is sewing silk of price and quality distancing foreign competition, yet it ought to be high-priced, for the duty of some 40 per cent. ought to add that much to its cost. Strange to say, it does not! The stuff has gone down instead of up!

WOOL AND WOOLENS.

From 1850 to 1860 the sheep in our country increased but little, only from 21,723,220 to 22,471,275. In 1861 the "Morrill tariff" was enacted, and in 1867 the protective duties on wools and woolens, which stood unchanged until 1883, were adopted. In 1870 we had 28,477,951 sheep, in 1880, 40,190,866. During these ten protective years a gain of 43 per cent. in sheep husbandry against a gain of a little over 3 per cent. from 1850 to 1860, and all this wool was bought by our own mills.

In 1860 these mills used 125,000,000 pounds, domestic and imported, 200,000,000 pounds in 1870, and 300,000,000 pounds, in round numbers, in 1880,—a healthy increase. In 1880 they bought of our wool growers, principally in the west and southwest, $100,000,000 worth, a single large factory using thirty thousand pounds, or six thousand fleeces, each day. Break down our 668 woolen mills in the Western States, and the 794 mills in the east, and the wool grower's market in London would be a poor one.

The wool growing interest in this country would suffer serious injury by any decrease in our home manufacture of woolens, as their clip increases each year and wants a growing home market from the manufacturers. These manufacturers would be equally injured by any decrease in the home supply of wool. Their interest is really one.

But are woolen goods higher, or lower, than in the low-tariff year 1860? The following table will show:

Goods.	1860.	1882.
Fitchburgh cassimeres, per yard...	.95 cents	.85 cents
Haile, Frost & Co., cashmerets....	.46 "	.38½ "
Men's ribbed socks, per doz........	8.00 "	4.50 "
Ladies' ribbed hose, "	4.25 "	3.00 "
Blankets, 9-4 Gonic..............	1.87½ "	1.75 "
" 10-4 "	2.37½ "	2.25 "
" 11-4 "	3.00 "	2.75 "
" 12-4 XX Rochdale.......	8.00 "	9.00 "
Moscow beavers, all-wool...	4.00 "	3.00 "
" " cotton-warp.....	1.35 "	1.00 "

"HONORABLE" IGNORANCE.

Mr. Titus Sheard, an Englishman by birth, now a woolen manufacturer, writes the following letter, criticising a gross misstatement:

To the Editor of the Commercial Bulletin:

In *Macmillan's Magazine* for February I find an article entitled "The Industries of the United States in Relation to the Tariff," by the Right Hon. Lyon Playfair, M. P.

Among the many curious statements I find the following, which is used to show how the poor man is ground down under our protective tariff:

"A workingman buying an ulster coat for the winter at Boston must pay double the price that an English workman does; that is, in Boston it costs eight pounds, and in England less than four.

"A workingman's woolen trousers in Boston cost seven shillings; a like pair in Manchester can be got for four."

Now, sir, is not this statement untrue; and an outrage upon the intelligent reader?

I do not know at what price you can get a pair of woolen trousers in Boston, but if you can get them for "seven shillings" you can get them in Boston as cheap as in Manchester, quality considered.

As to the ulster coat, we can buy them, all wool (not cotton warp), at $10 in our village—about two pounds, not "eight pounds;" so that they must cost much "less than four" pounds in England before they can buy as cheap there as here.

While I am writing, one of our workingmen, an Englishman, who has been in this country a little over one year, enters my office.

I read the above extract to him, and asked him how it is about the prices given and compared.

"Quality considered, I can buy as cheap here as I can at home in Yorkshire."

I asked him about the all-wool ulster coat which he had on, and how much it cost.

He answered, "ten dollars, and it aren't cotton warp, either."

"Is the suit of clothes you have on all wool?" "Yes, sir!" "What did they cost?" "Ten dollars." "What did those new shoes you have on cost?" "Two dollars and a-half." "Could you buy those clothes any cheaper at home?" "No, sir!"

"How about the shoes?" "They would cost me at home three dollars and a-half." "How about your stockings and shirt and underclothes?" "I can buy them as cheap here as at home!"

"What is there then here that costs you more than it would 'at home' for yourself or the support of your family?" "Nothing but house-rent and coals. Everything else is as cheap and in many cases cheaper. On the whole I can take better care of my family here, feed and clothe them better, and live more comfortably at the same cost than I can at home in England."

Nail this statement of facts to the mast of protection, as an answer to all the Right Hon. gentlemen, M. P.'s or otherwise, who choose to so misstate and misrepresent our industrial condition and deceive the workingmen of our own and other lands

Yours most respectfully,

TITUS SHEARD,

LITTLE FALLS, N. Y., April 4, 1882.

STAPLE CLOTHS CHEAP.

V. B. Denslow, of Chicago, says :

"I am informed by Mr. Marshall Field, the leading dry goods merchant in Chicago, * * that the prices at which ordinary cheap cottons and woolens sell in the United States are lower than in England. But in fine and costly goods we cannot compete with her in the markets of the world until we have her cheap labor, in some departments one-fourth the cost of ours, and we cannot have that cheap labor so long as we continue our protective tariff."

Hon. M. Haskill, M. C., of Kansas, in the tariff debate last winter in Washington, said :

"Then there is the article of woolen cassimere cloth. Take this great leading schedule or classification of woolen goods. Go back to your old comparative free-trade era from 1850 and 1860, when wool was free and the duty on cloth nominal. Take the case of the Hale & Frost factory, of Fitchburgh, Massachusetts, an old firm that was established in 1848, using the same old looms that were used from 1850 to 1860, hardly a new invention in their mills, the same old firm managing the business. Here are the Hale & Frost cashmerets, light wool spring goods, cotton warp, for men and boys ; with free wool and revenue tariff the prices of these goods from 1850 to 1860 averaged 51 cents per yard. Average price for the identical goods, made on same looms by same process in 1882, 45 cents per yard.

"Drawn from their books, I have a statement showing that from 1850 to 1860 they sold their cassimeres at an average price of $1.07 a yard. Then came the tariff rate under the law of 1861 ; and the duty, you say, is always added to the price. From 1870 to 1880, when we reached resumption, the Hale & Frost cassimeres averaged in price from their mill 97 cents a yard instead of $1.07.

"Take the very item of wool, in which you are all interested. From 1850 to 1860 wool was free, and the wool interests of this country were at a low ebb. The market for wool was in the hands of the importer ; it was in the hands of the foreign grower. To-day, under our tariff system, the market for American wool is in the hands of the American grower. Every pound of wool

The Free Trade Falsehood Refuted.

that the American farmer can raise he sells to-day to an American manufacturer, and the money stays at home—is not sent abroad. Do you say that the price of wool has increased under this tariff of 12 cents a pound as against the free wool of 1850 to 1860 ? I have here the figures. To-day wool is cheaper pound for pound, and has been for the last five years, than it was from 1855 to 1860 under the free rating of the free trade party."

Mr. SPRINGER. "Then what do you want a duty for ?

Mr. HASKELL. "Because, while the price of wool has fallen, the American grower holds the market and gets every dollar that the American wool manufacturer pays out for his material, except as to two items—clothing wool, a small importation, and carpet wools. I want the money paid by the manufacturer for wools to be paid in the United States, not in Australia, Africa, or Persia."

The Chicago *Morning Herald* tells of an Indiana woolen mill, the owner of which said, "from his books," that jeans which he sold at 60 cents per yard in 1860, brought him but 50 cents in 1874, while he paid higher wages at the last date than the first—price lower under a higher duty.

Mr. Archibald, English Consul General in New York, reported to his government: "The prices of carpets in the United States are 12 per cent. cheaper in 1879 than in 1860, while prices of dress goods have fallen about 25 per cent." This fact of falling prices under a higher tariff was thought of consequence enough to find place in a Parliamentary Report.

BRITISH FACTORY LIFE.

From Dewsbury, Yorkshire, England, Mr. Porter writes the *New York Tribune:*

"This is the centre of the woolen district in England. A circle of forty-five miles in diameter contains the greatest woolen and worsted regions in England. I might say of the world. Shoddy blankets, shoddy army cloths, and plushings and seal-skins are made here. The woolen factories are large gray stone buildings, walled in like prisons, with vigilant porters stationed at all the entrances lest strangers should accidentally get into the factories and appropriate the new designs or otherwise find out something of their internal economy. The manufacturers seem about as hard and sharp as the machines which weave their mungo and shoddy into cloth. The hands are ground down to the lowest penny, and a recent strike among the operatives brought out the fact that the average earnings of all hands, including the high-priced overseers and foremen was only sixteen shillings, or $4 a week at Dewsbury and Batley. The rent of one or two rooms in the poorest locality of the town, is £7 a year.

"These immense factories straggle along on the outskirts of Dewsbury for many miles."

The *London Standard* tells of 16,000 women and girls in "the Black Country" making nails, and "three or four persons working fourteen hours a day," and *earning, in all, five dollars a week*, living in wretched hovels, and the freshness of youth all crushed out."

Fortunately, British workers in some branches are better paid, and live better; but the average standard of life is far lower than here.

BRITISH SHODDY.

Honest excellence must be counted. The British common woolens and carpets have a great deal more shoddy in their fabrics than ours. Many of our mills use none. In a late speech in Congress Hon. W. D. Kelley said:

"What are shoddy and mungo? Why, sir, there is not a *chiffonnier* with stick and nail and bag scouring the gutters of any city on either side of the Atlantic for woolen rags who is not collecting material for the manufacture of shoddy and mungo. The cast-off clothing and the blankets which have wrapped putrefying carcasses in the lazar and pest-houses of Europe and Asia, are gathered and thrown into running streams whose waters are dammed at intervals, and when the law of gravitation and the flow of waters have made it safe to handle them they are collected and sent to Lancashire to be converted into shoddy cloths, flannels, blankets, and carpets. * * * * * *

"British carpets, we have been told, are much cheaper than ours. I hope the gentleman who represents the Macon (Georgia) district is on the floor. I want to mention a few facts which he can probably verify. The Bibb Manufacturing Company of Macon runs 11,000 spindles in the production of carpet-yarn. Mr. Hanson, the superintendent of the mill, sells all he can now produce to the carpet makers of Philadelphia, New York and New England. The capacity of the mill is to be greatly increased in order to meet the growing home demand for its yarn.

"But, impelled by fear that the duties on carpets would be reduced and his home market be thus destroyed, he addressed the most distinguished carpet manufacturer of England, sent him samples of his yarns, with price-list or tag attached to each parcel. His letter was courteously responded to, and with the answer came specimens of the yarns used by that distinguished carpet manufacturer in his immense works at Rochdale. The best of them did not equal the most inferior product of the Bibb Company, and John Bright stated candidly that such yarns as these could not be used by British carpet-makers, as they had to sell in countries in which low prices prevailed, and must consequently use the cheapest materials. No fresh cotton, said Mr. Hanson, could be found in any of those English carpet-yarns, and the lower grades were literally made of what might be called cotton shoddy, the waste of ordinary cotton mills."

THE POOR FARMER AND HIS BLANKETS.

In a speech in the West a few months ago Professor Percy spoke of the Iowa farmer who could buy two pair of blankets in England for what one pair would cost "in this privileged land," the tariff doubling the price to that poor farmer. This was assertion. Here is plain fact. The *Boston Commercial Bulletin* says:

"In order to determine the comparative prices of blankets in England and America, a pair of 5-lb. blankets was recently imported by a New England manufacturer at the lowest possible cost, the statement of their cost, duty-paid, was as follows:

"Cost of 1 pair of blankets received per steamship Batavia:
Cost at wholesale in England 18s. 1d., equal to.....$4.45
Weight duty. 5 pounds at 50c...............$2.50
Ad valorem do. 35 per cent.................. 1.75
———— 4.25
Custom house fees............................. .65
————
Total..$9.35

"Now, if it were true that the American price of an article is the English price plus the duties, such blankets ought to be selling here at $9.35 per pair; but as a matter of fact American blankets of precisely the same weight and quality are selling at $5.20 per pair, or but 75 cents higher than in England."

FLANNELS, ETC.

Flannels were high in 1880-2, but ten per cent. lower in 1878 than in 1860. Staple woolens for common working wear are cheaper. In the streets of Windsor, opposite Detroit, on the Canadian side of the river, are the handbills of our clothing merchants asking custom, and getting it, too. Our neighbors over the line are not stupid enough to come to us and pay higher for clothing than at home. This fact might be beneficial to the *Iowa State Leader*, which has been led by some of the notoriously loose assertions of D. A. Wells to say that the tariff has made woolens "outrageously dear to the consumer." A few days ago our daily papers reported the case of a Canadian woman caught in the effort to smuggle a pair of boots, bought here, for her own use. She forgot that they were taxed 35 per cent. by our "iniquitous tariff."

Mr. E. P. Brooks, U. S. Consul at Cork, Ireland, reports to the State Department at Washington, in August, 1881 : "Cheap clothing in the United States is cheaper than here. * * * Ireland has had free trade with England eighty years, during which time her woolen mills have been almost destroyed, yet her people buy their cheap clothing dearer than we pay."

The woolen manufacture of this country—cloths, carpets, worsted, and hosiery—in 1880 paid $45,959,000 wages; produced $234,589,671 worth; and used total raw material worth $145,141,000; (speech of Dr. G. B. Loring) increasing its products over $200,000,000 since 1840. Fear of this increase sends the poor cry across the ocean : "A tariff is a tax!" More than four-fifths of our woolen goods are made here, and the 50,000,000 consumers buy their working wear as cheap as in England, and are far more able to pay for it than the people there.

IRON AND STEEL.

Mr. John Roach says that the average price in New York of ship-plates, flange iron, angle iron and rivets, which he buys largely, was 25 per cent. lower, from 1870 to 1880, than from 1850 to 1860 under a lower tariff, and that wages were 20 per cent higher.

The *London Engineer*, devoted to British manufactures, says; "As far as the American consumer of iron is concerned he is the better off for protection." How can that protection tax the consumer?

Cast steel of English make had been sold here for twenty years, at 16 cents to 18 cents per pound, and none was made here. Under a higher tariff our steel makers began work about 1862, on a large scale, at Pittsburg and elsewhere, and the same quality came down to

13 cents and 15 cents. In the late civil war our cast steel was sold at 32 cents while British steel was held at 45 cents, thus saving our Government large sums in its war consumption, and saving us from dependence on a foreign power, always dangerous in such emergencies.

In a Congressional speech in April, 1881, Hon. Russell Errett, of Pittsburgh, stated that the English price of cast steel in New York, when they controlled our market and none was made here, was $17\frac{1}{4}$ cents per pound. That steel they now sell in Paris and other European markets for $12\frac{1}{4}$ cents, but in New York they sell it at $10\frac{1}{4}$ cents, making their price two cents lower in this country than in Europe, to break down our competition, or at least command a share of our market. His statement is confirmed by others. Plainly enough our home manufacture has largely reduced the price of steel, yet we are glibly told of "a tax of 60 per cent. on the consumers, imposed by our tariff!"

Mr. James Park, Jr., of the Black Diamond Steel Works, Pittsburgh, Pa., stated before the Congressional Naval Committee, in February, that extensive correspondence and inquiry led him to estimate the saving to users of cast steel in this country by the growth of our steel-making under a protective tariff, and the consequent reduction of price, at over $23,000,000, or 38 per cent. He said we paid higher wages than are paid abroad, and that no steel was superior to ours. Mr. Park is a man of large experience, and has visited all the great steel works of Europe.

STEEL RAILS.

Bessemer steel rails were first made in this country in 1867, but not largely until 1870. Up to the date of the opening of the first steel rail mill here the English controlled our market and prices, charging us $150 in gold per ton. The moment the first rails were made here they were compelled to reduce their prices, and brought them down in 1870 to $50.37 gold in England, equal to $57.93 in our currency. At that price they could be sent to New York and freight paid at a cost of $63 per ton, with no duty. Since then our American mills have furnished our railroads with over 3,000,000 tons, at an average cost of $59 per ton in currency, their prices going down from $106 in 1870 to $40 in the panic times of 1878, up to $85 in "the boom" of 1880, and now stand at $39 to $40. This great business employs over 20,000 American workmen, pays over $7,500,000 yearly in wages, and has furnished us steel rails for ten years at an average price *a little less* than the English price in 1870.

In the Western States $15,000,000 is invested in steel rail mills; their yearly product of nearly $20,000,000 is almost wholly raw material, labor and skill in our midst.

In the winter of 1879-80 officers of 15,300 miles of railroads asked Congress for a reduction of the duties to $10 per ton; but officers of 24,000 miles of railroads, with larger traffic (among them 6,000 miles going out from Chicago), asked the retention of that duty, on the ground that such a great reduction would be disastrous to them and to the makers of rails.

The English, thirty years ago, sold us immense quantities of "American rails"—so poor and brittle that that they could not be sold at home—at $50 per ton. In place of these we now have those of steel, safer and tenfold more durable, at $40. Here is a reminiscence of those days:

BROOKLYN, N. Y., February 15, 1882.
To the Secretary of the American Iron and Steel Association.

SIR : About the year 1850 the writer was a clerk in a house in Boston, which represented one of the largest of the English iron rolling mills. It was a period of low duties on railroad iron. The United States rail market was supplied partly from England and partly from American mills. The prices of rails were very low, and the English houses persisted in constantly depressing them, until, as this squeezing process went on, the American mills gradually shut down, and finally the last American mill was closed.

When the news from our house went across to England that there was no longer any danger from American competition, the reply immediately came back, "advance prices." This process of advancing prices then went on, until within less than a year prices to the American consumers had gone up nearly or quite 100 per cent., far beyond the price at which the home industries would gladly have supplied the demand had they been at work.
Yours Truly,
AN AMERICAN.

NAILS, SAWS AND AXES.

The manufacture of cut nails is an American invention, originating near the beginning of the present century. When it was first undertaken in this country, wrought nails, which then cost 25 cents a pound, were largely imported; hence the necessity for protection to the new industry. By the tariff act of 1824 the duty on all nails was made 5 cents per pound, at which it remained until 1833, since which year it has been reduced. Prices of cut nails have ranged as follows during the past fifty years: In 1828 the price was 7 to 8 cents per pound; in 1830·5 and 6 cents; from 1835 to 1840 from 5 to 7 cents, falling in 1840 to 5 and 6 cents; in 1844 and 1846 it was 4 and 5 cents; in 1861 it was 3 cents. Like all other products, the price advanced during the war, but before the panic of 1873 it had again fallen to 3 cents, and on the 1st of January, 1876, the price was $2\frac{1}{2}$ cents. It will be noted that, in 1830, six years after the duty was made 5 cents per pound, the price was the same as the duty; that, in 1833 the price fell below the duty; that, in 1842, it was 2 cents per pound below the duty; and that, on the 1st of January, 1876, it was just one-half the duty of 1824, and about one-fourth the price charged for cut nails when that duty was imposed. For a long time we have exported nails to foreign countries, the value of the exports of nails and spikes in the fiscal year 1875 amounting to half a million of dollars.

Prior to the revolution, and for many years after its close, our saws came from abroad, and we paid for them just what foreigners were pleased to charge us. In 1840 an American mechanic, Henry Disston, commenced the manufacture on a small scale. At that time English saws sold in our markets at from $15.75 to $19 a dozen. Mr. Disston was obliged to sell his saws for less money, as his goods were unknown; but after the Disston saw became known the English saws were gradually driven out of our markets and prices still further reduced. In 1876 Henry Disston & Sons were sending saws to England and selling them at $10.50 a dozen, fully fifty per cent. less than the price Englishmen charged us in 1840. When Mr. Disston commenced business, inferior saws of foreign manufacture were sold in this country at $4.50 a dozen, and he could not make saws for less than $7 a dozen, but now Henry Disston & Sons ship common saws to South America at $4.50. The exports of their goods in 1875 amounted to fully $100,000. The Messrs. Disston make their own steel.

Before axes were made in this country, except by country blacksmiths, English axes cost our farmers and others from $2 to $4 each. By the tariff of 1828 a protective duty of 35 per cent. was levied upon imported axes. Under this protection the Collins Company, of Hartford, introduced labor-saving machinery, much of which was invented, patented, and constructed by themselves. In 1836 foreign and home-made axes were selling side by side, in the American market, at $15 to $16 per dozen. Axes were selling, in 1838, at $13 to $15.25 per dozen; in 1843, at $11 to $12; in 1849, at $8 to $10. In 1876 the price of the best American axes in the market is $9.50 per dozen in currency, and the country exports to foreign markets. English writers admit their superior excellence. The Collins company makes its own steel, and a letter from the company claims that it is "better than any English steel we can buy, and we have been steel consumers for fifty years. We now only make for our own consumption, and we have no disposition to cheat ourselves."—*American Iron Trade.*

CUTLERY.

In 1842, President Wayland of Brown University, Providence, R. I., said (Political Economy, page 140) :

"We pay a heavy duty on cutlery in this country, while not a thousandth part of the cutlery used is made here. It would be vastly cheaper to pay a bounty sufficient to raise all the cutlery made in this country to its present prices, and it would be, for aught I see, just as good for the cutler."

He was an estimable gentleman, but like some other college professors, was a theorist ignorant of the facts of industrial life.

If the American people had listened to him they would not have the cheap and abundant supply of hardware and cutlery that they enjoy at this time. Forty years ago American hardware was almost unknown in the trade, yet five-sixths of the consumption is now supplied by home industry, and our exported cutlery is on the shelves of dealers in Sheffield and Birmingham.

In 1842, Wayland thought it ridiculous to protect the American manufacturers of these goods, but the "high duty" produced results which he could not foresee. What they are let an English journal tell.

Ryland's *Iron Trade Circular*, for March 4, 1871, at Birmingham, England, says:

"The edged-tool trade is well sustained, and we have less of the effects of American competition. That this competition is severe, however, is a fact that cannot be ignored. The ascendance of the protectionist party in the States continues to operate most favorably for the manufacturing interest there, and it is no wonder that, under such benignant auspices, the enterprise in this direction is swelling to colossal proportions."

In a speech in the United States Senate, February 27, 1832, George M. Dallas, who became Vice-President under James K. Polk, gave his personal knowledge regarding the effects of the protective tariffs of 1824 and 1828 in cheapening the prices of various articles manufactured from iron or steel:

"The reduction of the prices was a necessary consequence of the domestic competition created and excited by the policy.

Since 1818, 1819, and 1820 the implements of husbandry have sunk in price thus: Axes, from $24 to $12 by the dozen; scythes, spades, and common shovels, 50 per cent. Iron hoes, at $9 by the dozen, have given way to steel ones at $4. Socket shovels, once sold at $12 a dozen, now sell at $4.50; iron vises, once at 20 cents by the pound, now at 10 cents; braziers' rods were, in 1821, imported at $313 by the ton, and now are made at $130; and steam-engines have actually, since 1828, fallen 50 per cent. in price, while at the same time the amount of material and labor of which they are composed has nearly doubled."

Facts like these are worth tons of theories concocted by scholars who get all their knowledge from books, rather than go out into the actual world.

Let all the schoolboys cypher out how a tariff is a tax on nails, saws, axes, and cutlery. It will be a tough job; perhaps they will have to take their slates home from school and get their fathers to help them; and perhaps the fathers will give it up.

SALT.

Deluded dairymen resolve that the salt monopoly must be destroyed, and the fearful salt tax in the shape of a tariff, under which they suffer, must be abolished. An Illinois dairyman said in a convention that three-fourths of an ounce of salt to a pound of butter was enough. Call it six pounds of salt to one hundred pounds of butter, suppose the tariff of 12 cents on 100 pounds of imported salt is a tax, and when the groaning dairyman sells his nice firkin of a hundred pounds of butter, and pockets his $20 or more, he has paid a tax of three-fourths of a cent! But he has sold his salt, which cost him say 6 cents, for over $1.20, and still he groans about the tax! The revenue of a million dollars or more which the salt tariff yields to the government

The Free Trade Falsehood Refuted. 73

even if the whole duty is added to the price, would average about five cents per head of our total population. A fearful tax!

But its price in Chicago, where the west gets its largest supply, is about a dollar a barrel (280 pounds, or five bushels, barrel included) or half the cost in 1860.

Here are the prices at Saginaw, where 3,000,000 barrels a year are made:

Average price per barrel, 1866		$1 80
"	" 1868	1 85
"	" 1870	1 32
"	" 1872	1 46
"	" 1874	1 19
"	" 1876	1 05
"	" 1878	85
"	" 1880	75
"	" 1882	74

PLATE GLASS.

At St. Louis, Mr. E. A. Hitchcock stated to the Tariff Commission that the yearly production of American plate glass was about two million square feet, or half the consumption; that labor represented near three-fourths of its cost; that the average duty for fifteen years had been about fifty per cent.; and that *the cost had been reduced in ten years from $2.50 to $1.00 per square foot.*

LUMBER.

The Iowa farmer groans over the moderate duty of 15 to 20 per cent. on lumber, as adding $2 per thousand feet to the price he pays. Had he studied the Chicago prices current he would know that for the three years from 1863 to 1865, with Canada lumber free, the average yearly prices were *not any lower* than in the three years from 1867 to 1869, when the duty was 20 per cent. Some times this might be different, but this shows that the duty was not added to the price of the thousands of millions of feet of lumber sent over the West in those years. It may be asked, Why then do our lumber manufacturers want a duty on imported lumber? Not that it so much affects the price, as they furnish the larger part, but that the duty lessens the imports, gives them a wider market, helps to give employment to 200,000 workmen, at wages 25 per cent. higher than in Canada, and to keep up a home market for $30,000,000 of the products of our farms and $20,000,000 of home manufactures which they consume each year.

A FRENCH STATEMENT.

In 1878 a French Senatorial Commission to examine their trade and its relations to other nations, said, in their report: "A veritable economical revolution has taken place in the United States. Under the shelter of a prohibition system * * they have organized a powerful industry *which rivals England in cheapness.*" We "rival England in cheapness," the impartial foreigners say; yet free traders here pretend that our tariff adds 30 to 60 per cent. to our prices!

BOOTS AND SHOES.

Would the buyers of boots and shoes be helped if $43,000,000 of yearly wages were paid to workmen in foreign lands, and $166,000,000 worth of these articles brought in from abroad instead of being made at home, and sold in our shoe stores as cheap as in English retail shops?

PAPER—"A TAX ON KNOWLEDGE."

"A tax on knowledge" is what free traders call the moderate duty of 20 per cent. on printing paper. A great cry was raised about it all at once in 1879. Suppose it is a tax added to the price of paper. It would add *four cents a year* to the cost of a seven-column weekly newspaper! In war days, with paper at 25 cents per pound, daily papers sold at about their present prices. Did newspapers reduce their rates in 1879, while getting their paper of our manufacturers at less than 6 cents—half what it cost in 1872? In 1872-3 the price was 12 cents; it fell gradually to 6 cents and less in the depression of 1879, rose to 10 cents in "the boom" of 1880, and is now down to 6½ to 7 cents, with the duty unchanged. If the tariff is responsible for the rise, why not credit it with the fall as well?

How came this sudden hue and cry about "a tax on knowledge?" The circulars that filled the land had all the same "ear-marks," as coming from one centre. A Yankee guess would put it at free trade headquarters in New York.

Englishmen tell us that *we* pay all the duty on the goods they send us, but at home they tell each other how *they* are taxed by our tariff. Their statement is like the almanac—"adapted to the latitude." Canadians, when asking for reciprocity, told at home how *they* had to pay the duty on their coal, wool, lumber, and barley, exported to the United States. This side the line we were told that the same duty was a *tax on us*.

RICE—A SOUTHERN CONGRESSMAN.

In the House of Representatives. January, 1883, Hon,

E. Speer, M. C., of Georgia, member of the Ways and Means Committee, made the following remarks:

MR. SPEER.—I wish to say to the gentleman from Illinois [Mr. Sparks] that there are many ways in which this system of protection protects the farmer. I will give one instance in reference to the rice-planters of Georgia and the Carolinas. Before the war rice was worth $2 a hundred. When the war came our whole system of labor was disorganized and the rice interest was swept out of existence. After the war, before the interest was built up by protection, the price of rice per hundred in this country was from $12 to $14. The tariff had its beneficial effect on that interest, and what is the consequence? Our rice interest is built up again, from 160,000 to 200,000 people are engaged in profitable agricultural occupation, and rice, instead of being from $12 to $14 per hundred, is now only $4.25 to $4.50.

LOOSE AND RECKLESS ASSERTIONS.

Mr. David A. Wells of Connecticut, a noted free trade authority, formerly a protectionist, and a disciple of Henry C. Carey, made a Western tour a few years ago, and spoke in our leading cities. In Detroit he held up before his audience a table-knife of American manufacture, praised the skill and fine machinery used by our cutlery makers, but regretted they were "taxed 60 per cent. on the steel they use by the tariff." Up to 1859 English steel had varied little for twenty years from 10 cents, 12½ cents and 16 cents for different grades, *the English controlling our market and prices.*

With a protective duty our steel makers took away that foreign control by their competition, and 9 cents, 10½ cents and 13 cents were prices for the same grades. How could Mr. Wells ignore these facts? Is he so ignorant as not to know that our cutlery competes with that of free trade England, the world over?

Professor Perry left his place in Williams College last spring to visit the West and enlighten the people. He told us that the "farmer is virtually prohibited from selling his hogs outside his own country by our absurd tariff." By the U. S. Agricultural Report for 1880 the exports of hogs, bacon and hams were $61,331,629. The farmers can stand a good deal of such prohibition.

Professor Sumner of Yale rivals his brother teacher from Williams in loose assertions. He lately said, as the *Philadelphia Press* reports, that "hundreds of poor women worked hard for fifty cents a day" in the Willimantic spool thread mills, while, in fact, none work there for such poor pay, and their average earnings are double that sum.

Thomas G. Shearman, an attorney in Brooklyn, N. Y., came to Detroit last winter to lecture on free trade. I heard him say: "The worst cloth in the world is made in the United States. * * No good woolens are made in America," and noted the words at the time.

Against his assertion I put the impartial statement of a foreign expert. M. Louis Chatel was the French Government Commissioner to our Centennial Exhibition in 1876 at Philadelphia, especially to study spinning and weaving. In his report to that government he said: "The Americans can justly claim a very large share in the progress attained (in woolens) at the present day," and this progress, especially in staple goods "for general consumption, has done serious injury to the markets of England and France." He especially commended the cloths of the Globe Woolen Company of Utica, N. Y., for "perfectness in weaving and finish," and said: "We are forced to admit that our manufacturers of Vienne and of Bischmiller (famed French mills) can no longer compete, either in cost or quality, with the goods of this American company." Washington Mills, Lawrence, Mass., and others, were also highly commended.

Of these Globe Mill woolens over $600,000 worth were sold in New York city in 1882—beautiful goods, costing, some of them, over five dollars per yard at wholesale. Comment is needed on this striking contrast. So far as staple goods are concerned, one case of many may be instanced. Any merchant in our city will readily grant that, for honest wear, the cassimeres of the Flint Woolen Mills, in our own State, are genuine and excellent.

"THE CONSOLATIONS OF THE PROTECTED FARMER"— A CANADIAN VIEW.

The New York Free Trade League a few years ago circulated a sheet entitled "The People's Pictorial Taxpayer," purporting to illustrate, by various cartoons and pictures, the baleful effect of levying a tax on such foreign products as compete with our own. Conspicuously displayed on the borders of this sheet were the cards of Wm. Jessup & Sons, manufacturers of steel and importers of iron, Sheffield, England; of Congreve & Son, of New York, agents of the Toledo Steel Works, of Sheffield; of A. B. Sands & Co., importers of drugs; of John Clark, Jr., & Co., foreign manufacturers of spool-cotton; of Van Wart & McCoy, the New York agents of Van Wart, Son & Co., of Birmingham, and a dozen other English manufacturing firms and their agents in New York. Besides these are the cards of several foreign insurance companies. A noble set of backers, these, to teach American tax payers their true interests!

The principal cartoon is entitled, "How the tariff robs the farmer and every workingman to benefit the monopolists."

Our Canadian neighbors were then discussing a protective tariff to shield themselves from the philanthropic free trade of the mother country, which they have since adopted. *The Toronto Mail*, an able advocate of protection for Canadian industry, took up this Pictorial Tax-payer, and other like sheets in the United States, and commented on them under the head of "Consolations of the Protected Farmer," in a keen and clear way, as follows:

"The Yankee farmer rises in the morning tolerably refreshed. True, he has been sleeping on a bed, the sheets, blankets, and mattresses of which would have been taxed from 60 to 180 per cent. had they been imported from a foreign country. But they are home-made, and his dreams have not been disturbed by the free trade bugbear that 'protection raises the price of the home manufactured article up to at least the price of the imported article *plus* the import duty.' Mr. David A. Wells and other agents of the Leeds and Manchester manufacturers once tried to frighten him with this bogy; but experience has taught him that it is only a make-believe. There is an import duty of 8 cents a yard on cotton sheeting, but he buys it from the cotton factory in his market town at 7 cents a yard, and sees it going to England in competition with free trade cotton. Moreover, he knows that it is to that import duty he owes the establishment of the neighboring cotton factory, whose operatives give him a profitable home market for rotation crops. He is well satisfied with his bed. It is home-made; it cost him, if anything, less than an imported article; and its manufacture has given employment to artisans who buy the products of his farm almost direct from his wagon.

"He is not alarmed because there is a heavy import duty on foreign cloths, boots, and cotton shirts. His suit from head to foot is of American make; he thinks this is better for him than if his coat had come from the west of England, his shirt from Manchester, and his boots from Stockport.

Breakfast over, he takes to his farm implements. Foreign implements, such as shovels, hoes, wooden pails, churns, reapers, etc., are taxed 35 per cent. ; and in 1860, when the battle of the Morrill tariff was being fought in Congress, the agents of the great Bedford and Leicester firms predicted that an import duty on their goods would ruin farming in the United States. He has discovered that this is not true, and that Yankee farm implements have become the cheapest and best in the world. In fact, when our farmer contemplates the amazing growth of this industry, it occurs to him that the English agents, who lobbied and even bribed politicians and newspapers to oppose the high tariff, were not actuated so much by regard for the condition of the Yankee farmer as by the consciousness that protection would deprive them of the American market, and by the fear that it would make the Yankee manufacturer a formidable rival in other markets.

"This is what the farmer thinks at his work during the forenoon. He hears the toot of the dinner horn, and sits down at the table nothing put out by the reflection that tin horns of foreign make are taxed about two cents each. Neither does he lose his appetite when he remembers that furniture, such as the chair he is sitting on, the table at which he is eating, is taxed 35 per cent. when of foreign make. This duty has helped to establish furniture factories and to give employment to tens of thousands of mechanics at home, and in this way has benefited him.

"After dinner he sets out for the market town, and, as he journeys thither, he pities the Canadian farmer, who, as a rule, has to dispose of his produce to the middlemen that stand like a row of tax-gatherers, each levying his tithe between the Kanuck farm and the foreign consumer. He wonders, too, does this old Yankee farmer, how the Canadian farms endure wheat and barley year after year, and rejoices that protection has given him a home market to which he can supply almost every variety of crop. He enters the market town at one o'clock, and his sympathy for the Canadian farmer is deepened as he sees troops of Canadian operatives returning to the factories from their dinner.

"'I wonder,' he communes, 'if the Kanuck farmer ever sees a crowd of Yankee operatives going to work in a Canadian factory? Guess not. Then what do free traders mean by arguing that protection, such as we Yankies are cursed with, ruins industry, while free trade, with which the Kanucks have long been blessed, builds it up and makes a nation great? If that were so, would not these active little French-Canadians be at work in Montreal, and would not our Yankee mechanics be pouring over there also?'

"By this time he has reached the store, and disposes of his tomatoes, potatoes, etc. With the money received in payment he makes his little purchases, and finds no small consolation in knowing that almost every dollar he pays out goes to home industries.

"He thinks this over as he travels homeward, and talks protection vs. free trade with his sons in the evening. One of them works on the farm, and the others are at trades in the town— Canada has had no attractions for them. 'You boys are all here,' says the old man, 'and I guess it is a pretty good country, protection and all.'"

CHEMICALS.

By the tenth census we had 1,346 factories, with $85,336,856 invested; annual sales of $117,128,657; employing 29,435 hands in this industry; using 586,089 tons of coal, and consuming raw materials worth $79,237,281 yearly.

In Philadelphia and New York alone the yearly manufacture of chemicals reaches $50,000,000. Look at a few facts in that line. On flower of sulphur the duty equals 59 per cent., its price abroad 4 cents per pound. With the duty added as "a tax," it should sell for 6 cents, but it only brings 3 cents in our market. Refined borax, sold abroad at 14 cents, with a duty of 10 cents, should bring 24 cents here, but home competition keeps it down to 14 cents. Chloroform is too sleepy to go up to $1.37½, where the "tariff is a tax" theory would send it, but is dull at 75 cents. Castor oil sells abroad at 9¼ cents to 9⅔ cents per pound, and the duty is rated at equal to 148 per cent., which would bring it up to 22 to 23 cents here; but it sells at 12½ to 15 cents. Epsom salts, with its foreign price of $1\tfrac{3}{10}$ cents and the duty or "tax" of 78 per cent. added, should sell at $2\tfrac{3}{10}$ cents, but does not rise above 1⅖ cents per pound, even to meet free trade nonsense. Strychnine ought to sell at $1.95 per ounce, but it holds fast at only 80 cents.

FARMERS THE GREATEST "MONOPOLISTS"—THE NONSENSE OF IT!

Nothing so completely shows the absurdity of the "tariff is a tax" assumption as to apply it to farm products. In 1870 we imported 190,000 bushels of potatoes, which paid a duty of fifteen cents per bushel, or $28,500. We raised 240,000,000 bushels, and on this whole crop the price was raised, if this assumption be correct, fifteen cents per bushel by this "tax" on the imported product. This logic taxes the poor people who raise no potatoes $36,000,000 in that one year for the benefit of a few greedy grangers!

In 1878, in a congressional speech, Hon. W. D. Kelley gave the following table:

Products.	Bushels Raised in 1877.	Bushels Exported.	Home Consumption. Bushels.	Duty per bushel.	Tax on home consumers by the Free Trade dogma that the duty is added to the price.
Wheat......	360,000,000	57,043,936	302,956,064	$0 20	$60,591,212 80
Barley......	35,600,000	1,186,936	34,413,871	15	5,162,080 65
Potatoes....	146,000,000	529,650	145,470,350	15	21,820,522 50
Corn	1,340,000,000	73,100,518	1,266,899,482	10	126,689,948 20
Oats........	405,000,000	2,854,128	402,145,872	10	40,214,587 20
Rye	22,100,000	2,227,000	19,873,000	10	1,987,300 00
Total......	2,308,700,000	136,941,361	2,171,758,639		$256,465,681 35

How we all suffer, that these grain growers may gain $250,000,000 yearly at our cost! Include dairy products, and meats, grant that the producers use one-third and sell the rest, and we are taxed over $350,000,000 yearly to fatten these rapacious farmers! Can absurdity go farther? The fact is the tariff on these products makes no difference with their price, yet pays a good revenue to the government.

Sometimes the admission of a competitor covers the whole ground. In 1879 Col. Wrottlesey, an Englishman, wrote the *London Times:* "The Americans have the start of us, * * and unless our manufacturers bestir themselves they will completely command the markets of Europe." Mr. McHardy, in his report to Parliament as one of the British commissioners to the Centennial Exhibition at Philadelphia in 1876 said: "It is foolish not to recognize the fact that at Philadelphia, Great Britain was in face of her most powerful rival in manufactures." How is this rivalry possible unless our qualities and prices compete with theirs in foreign lands? If our tariff is a tax, added to the price of our goods how is such competition possible?

Added evidence of the absurd folly and falsehood of this free trade assertion is abundant but needless; what is given is impregnable, its disproval impossible.

Bear in mind that this assertion is intended to give the idea that the amount of any duty is so much always added, not only to the price of the imported article, but to the price of all like articles made in this country and that this added burthen falls on the consumer here, who is thus craftily and heavily robbed for the benefit of protected monopolists.

Hon. H. G. Turner, M. C., of Georgia, in a late speech

estimated the added cost to consumers caused by the tariff at $1,000,000,000,—so much profit to our manufacturers while the government gets less than $200,000,000, and Hon. W. R. Cox, M. C., of North Carolina, figures it up that government gets $104,000,000 revenue from duties on cotton and woolen goods, iron and steel, and leather imported, but the makers here get $553,414,000. Start from false premises and it is easy work to make a false case.

These men, and their like, *have no ground of fact to stand on.* A Hindoo theory is that this earth stands on the back of an enormous elephant, and that each of his feet rests on the back of an immense tortoise. Ask the grave Hindoo pundit what the four tortoises stand on, and he shakes his head solemnly, but gives no light. He is in dim fog and chaos, where these men reach when facts are called for. Assumption is the free trade tortoise. standing solid on—nothing !

CHAPTER VII.

A TARIFF FOR REVENUE ONLY TAXES THE CONSUMER—DUTIES—PRICES.

Those who assert that a protective tariff is a tax on the consumer make that assertion the ground for advocating a tariff for revenue only. By that advocacy they uphold the very tax they so stoutly denounce. Revenue duties on tea, coffee, and other articles we cannot produce, and on which there can be no home competition, tend to raise their price. The English consider the duty on tea as a permanent tax on the people of some 20,000,000 yearly. The more we act on the free trade "axiom" that protection taxes the consumer the more we shall frame our tariffs for revenue only, and thus tax that consumer permanently.

Briefly stated, the case is as follows: A tariff for revenue only is a permanent tax on the consumer, with no compensating benefits. A protective tariff pays the surest revenues to our government, is sometimes a transient tax, but always has compensating benefits from the start, and always results in low prices,—being thus a boon rather than a tax.

Experience and the laws of trade show that when we have any well established industry producing the greater part of what we consume, this home product controls our prices, home competition cheapens them, and the foreigner pays the duty, which does not affect the price. Imported cotton cloth, for instance, affects prices little, if any. When we make any article, and import a large share of what we use of the like article, sometimes the foreigner pays the duty and sometimes we pay a part, or supply and demand fluctuate, *but our competition with the foreign maker always reduces prices.* A protective duty on a new industry may sometimes keep the price up for a short time; sometimes the foreigner reduces his price to cripple our new industry, and we reap the benefit,—as in the case of steel rails, on which English prices were reduced some $20 per ton as soon as they were made here.

Whenever an article of home manufacture happens to be dearer than a like foreign article the difference is surely held up as a tax on the consumer, caused by the duty, but when home competition brings the price down, as it has done in many cases, that is ignored. To point back to *higher* prices under *lower* duties would greatly damage a free trade treatise. Home competition, home markets, better wages, varied employment and capital used at home are silently passed by; to exaggerate alleged injuries and ignore real benefits is the aim. The process by which manufacturers are shown to gain immense profits is equally incorrect and untrue. Sometimes a factory pays nothing to its owner for years and then come good dividends. The years without profit are ignored, but the good dividend is paraded and magnified to keep up prejudices against "the monopolists." Hon. W. A. Russell, M. C., gives the reports of fifty-one textile manufactories known in Boston, showing their dividends for ten years, from 1873 to 1882 inclusive, to be $6\frac{8}{10}$ per cent. yearly average on $55,000,000 capital. Approximately it would be safe to say that for thirty years our factories and mills in the whole country have not paid their owners five per cent. yearly. Many cases can be given where a single crop has paid for the farmer's land and labor. Would it be fair to hold them up as proofs that those farmers are constantly getting rich at the cost of the consumers of food?

Start any new industry, with fair protection, and it gains and grows and these results follow :—better processes and machinery, economy of production, less cost of manufacture on a larger scale, ability sometimes to pay more for raw material and for wages, yet to sell the product lower, and a rise in the price of lands in the vicinity along with the growing cheapness of the product of the mill.

THE OLD STORE AND THE NEW.

Suppose there is a great store on some country road where all the people have been obliged to trade, and a new shop starts across the highway. Galled and fleeced by the monopoly of the old store they patronize the new one to get the benefits of a healthy competition.

Our fifteen hundred woolen mills are the new store on our side of the (ocean) highway. How competition with the old shop, kept by a solid Englishman on the other side, has worked may be shown by a word from Hon. W. S. Shallenberger, of Pennsylvania, who spoke on behalf of the National Association of Wool Growers at the New York Tariff Convention in November, 1881. He said : "On the subject of domestic clothing, I desire to add a word. While it is true that the price of fine broadcloth is cheaper in Europe than here, our staple cloth can be furnished to the workingman for less than such cloth costs abroad. I rely on the statement of no less a person than the Quartermaster-General of the United States army for the information that the clothing of that army, when quality is considered, is cheaper than that of any army in the world. There is an intelligent gentleman sitting here by me who has traveled around the world in a suit of clothing (coat, vest and pants) costing $12, the quality of which has been commented on by foreigners all over the world as being remarkable."

Reduce the product of these woolen mills, and it would be like the country merchant in the new store being obliged to lessen the quantity and variety of his stock. The old store across the road would get more trade *and better profit at the cost of the people.*

Our prices are not always as low as in Europe. Bring wages down from thirty to a hundred per cent., or to the British and European level, and we could undersell the world. Shall we brutalize our people to do that? To drag man down that iron may be cheap, would be a crime and a blunder.

But the great staples used by the people grow cheaper under protection. The British sometimes admit that the users of iron among us are the better off for our policy,— and that means everybody, for iron is used in hut and palace, on the farm and in the shop. The woolens most used are as cheap as abroad, while finer goods, luxuries for those who buy them, are higher. Almost a third of our customs-duties comes from the tariff on textile fabrics, cottons and woolens pay a large part of it, and a good share of that the foreigner pays without affecting our prices. Even if a tariff is a tax, since we prosper more with protection than with revenue tariffs on the free trade plan, we had better pay it and take the good results as abundant compensation.

On the broad scale, however, there is no doubt that the growth of our protected manufactures gives us better goods at lower cost than we should pay without these useful home industries. Facts prove this, and that proof stamps the free trade assertion that a tariff is a tax on the consumer as an assumption without evidence.

We must bear in mind that without protective tariffs our great industries could not have grown to their present magnitude, or our country have reached its present wealth. Our manufactures, by the last census, were $5,369,000 in 1880, mostly used at home. It is a vast attainment of these industries to reach the capacity of such large supplies for our home wants. Suppose they were reduced one-fourth. We should be compelled to pay foreigners, mostly British, $1,300,000,000 yearly; our balance of trade would turn against us; gold would flow out to Europe; bonds go abroad for market; farmers' home markets and prices languish; wages fall, and imported goods rise, and a period of panic and bankruptcy follow.

A PROTECTIVE TARIFF LIKE A LEVEE OR A FENCE.

Why need a tariff at all on articles in which we can compete with the world, and on which foreign importers pay the duty if they are brought here? There will always be imports of special styles of goods, and a duty on them will yield needed revenue to our government. We want a duty, also, as a barrier against possible importations made with a purpose and to our injury. When Prussia, in 1818, established some protective duties, a member of the British Parliament advocated flooding that country with British goods, even at a sacrifice.

David Syme, an able English free trader, went to Australia and saw there the workings of a policy which led the people of that British colony to adopt a protective tariff. He frankly said :

"The manner in which English capital is used to maintain her manufacturing supremacy is well understood abroad. In any quarter of the globe where a competition shows itself as likely to interfere with her monopoly, immediately the capital of her manufacturers is massed in that particular quarter, and goods are exported in large quantities and sold at such prices that outside competition is effectually counted out. English manufacturers have been known to export goods to a distant market and sell them under cost for years, with a view to getting the market into their own hands again."

This is the British avowed policy, "to gain and keep foreign markets and step in for the whole trade when prices revive."

Sometimes it is good policy for foreign manufacturers, when their markets at home are glutted, to send goods here, even at a loss, and reap the benefit by relieving their nearer marts of a surplus. To this Hon. A. S. Hewitt, of New York, alluded in saying: "These duties have conferred one great benefit. In the late era of depression (1873, etc.), they have prevented this country from being the sink into which the surplus iron of other countries would be flung. Had the duties been low enough iron importations would have destroyed our business and closed our establishments."

Such closing would have raised prices by making us dependent on foreigners. Even the reduction of our duties sometimes raise prices abroad. In 1870, when the tariff on pig iron was reduced $2 per ton, the Scotch makers at once added that sum to the price.

In 1880 the mere proposal in Congress, by a bill which

did not pass, to reduce largely the duty on steel rails, sent the price up in England ten dollars in three days.

"The *Minneapolis Wood and Iron*," a journal from the new and beautiful manufacturing city by the Falls of St. Anthony, makes this excellent comparison:

"The mechanic, trader, farmer, or manufacturer who desires a removal of the protective tariff may be compared to an inhabitant of the low-lying lands bordering on the Mississippi river who advocates cutting the levee which protects him and his possessions from the hungry flood without. With the levee in good condition labor is rewarded by increase, and prosperity reigns. Destroy it, and decay takes the place of fruitful growth, and haggard poverty reigns instead of smiling plenty. Let the dwellers behind the barrier of protection examine it closely and watch it constantly. It may be too strong in some places, in others too weak; but as they value their lives let them preserve its stability unimpaired. Then, as the dwellers behind the levee use the broad waters beyond for the transportation of themselves and their products wheresoever they will, so the nation safely intrenched behind its tariff sea-wall can venture forth to trade and grow rich throughout the earth, secure in the thought that return when they may they will find the fields left behind as blooming and fertile as when they bade them farewell."

A witty man being asked: "What is the use of a duty higher than the article really needs?" answered in the Yankee fashion by asking a question: "What is the use of a fence higher than the field it encloses?"

WHY DO WE NOT EXPORT MANUFACTURES LARGELY?

This question is often asked, honestly or captiously. The answer is easy. Only a hundred years ago, we escaped from the grasp of that British power that had always crushed our manufactures, and one of whose eminent men (Lord Chatham, in 1772), declared that "the colonists should not be allowed to make a hobnail for themselves." We started poor and without manufactures. For a long time every new industry had a struggle for life through the varying and uncertain legislation of inexperienced men, and from want of capital. In this single century we have reached a product of over $5,369,000,000 in 1880, supplying nine-tenths of the wants of fifty million people, the greatest buyers, per head, in the world. Our population grows two millions annually, and our manufactures must increase over $200,000,000 a year to supply this large addition to our numbers. Nothing in the industrial progress of the world equals this great achievement of our single century of peaceful industry! And, beyond even this, we export to distant countries. England's very life depends on a great export trade in her manufactures; our life grows sure and strong and we first supply our vast and increasing home demand. Let us do that, and our exports will dispose of our surplus.

CHAPTER VIII.

SOME FREE TRADE FALLACIES ANSWERED.

It has been shown that free trade efforts in this country are heartily approved by the classes in England who expect to gain most profit from their success. It is also significant that the staple assertions of free trade theorists with us are of English origin, and have long been common in that country, showing an inspiration here drawn from "the fast anchored isle" across the Atlantic. Let us look at a few of these assertions.

"PROTECTION WILL FETTER AND DECREASE EXPORTS AND IMPORTS."

The assumption is that people abroad will not buy of us while we put tariff barriers in the way of their selling to us. Our great foreign trade, with its aggregate of $1,499,901,099 in 1880, an increase of some $500,000,000 in ten years, growing under a protective tariff and larger for these years than ever before, refutes that assertion.

Look back and we shall find our exports and imports increased in our protective periods and grew less whenever we approached the "tariff for revenue only" policy.

Our exports to Great Britain in 1879 were over $500,000,000, our imports $100,000,000. They bought our grain, cotton and provisions because they needed them, and our duties on their articles did not stand in the way. We buy coffee from Brazil, tea from China and sugar from Cuba largely, because we want them, but these countries do not buy of us half as much as we do from them.

Let us see how an able English protectionist meets this assertion in that country. Sir J. B. Byles, in his "Sophisms of Free Trade," which has passed through ten editions in England, said in 1880 : "Our answer to this assertion is an appeal to facts. No nation has adopted the theory and practice of protection to the same extent as England; no nation has, at the same time, enjoyed so extensive and lucrative a foreign trade. For centuries the greatest protection in the world has coincided with the greatest foreign trade in the world. In truth, the domestic activity, industry and prosperity, fostered by the protective system, is the surest basis of a permanent, extensive and mutual foreign trade. In the first place, with protection and a certain home market, have arisen *the means of purchase.* Under a strict and jealous system of protection we have seen the rise of Manchester, Birmingham, Sheffield, Bradford, and other cities. We have seen skill and machinery brought to perfection. Protection has not blunted the invention or superseded the ingenuity of our countrymen. On the contrary, our cottons and woolens and hardware *were* the best in the world. What England might have been *without* protection from foreign manufactures, we know not. She might have been what Ireland is now without protection from English manufactures. But it is certain that *with* protection the means of purchase have been created and multiplied in a degree marvellous and transcending all anticipation. * * With protection has arisen the indispensable pre-requisite to foreign trade—things to give in exchange for foreign commodities, the means of purchase—exports."

Some Free Trade Fallacies Answered. 95

"PROTECTED MANUFACTURES HAVE A SICKLY AND HOT-BED GROWTH."

With this assertion come pictures of growing oranges under hot-house glass in Scotland, of raising figs in warm rooms in Maine, and all sorts of foolish things for thoughtless people to laugh at. Look at facts, and surely we see nothing but vigor and benefit in the great industries of our land. Our woolen mills buy all the wool of our sheep growers. Our iron and steel mills, with the manufactures therefrom, and the allied ore and coal products, employ some 650,000 persons (estimate in 1870 of Iron and Steel Association, in Philadelphia). These and other industries makes a larger and better home market for farm products than ever opened abroad. Nothing sickly in all this.

Let us see how the English writer shows up this sophistry.

"All our British manufactures took their rise in a system of protective duties so high as to amount to prohibition." "They are the greatest, and, until lately, the least sickly of any." "Protection to French industry, from the days of Colbert, has been and will be the policy of France. Her manufactures, though inferior to ours, have augmented, since peace, in an even greater ratio, but under strict protection." Look at Russia. Mr. Cobden has recently visited their protected textile manufactures. According to him, these manufactures, which should have been sickly and stunted according to these theories, now threaten a rivalry with Great Britain." "In every instance of nations adopting the protective system, manufactures have been *created*, not sickly, but healthy and flourishing, often against natural disadvantages. In all cases industry has been forced into an artificial channel; but the result has been solid and prodigious prosperity."

"BUY IN THE CHEAPEST MARKET."

A tariff stands in the way of this, we are told, and is therefore, at best, only a necessary evil to be got out of the way as soon as possible. A witty Irishman in this country was telling how cheap goods were in his old home, and how much he could buy there for a sixpence. "Why did you come here then?" he was asked. "And shure, where could I get the sixpence at home?" was his quick reply. He burst the bubble of "cheapest market." Free trade fails to put the sixpences into people's pockets.

"THE PURCHASE OF FOREIGN ARTICLES, IF CHEAPER THAN THOSE AT HOME, SO MUCH CLEAR GAIN."

Adam Smith, the apostle of free trade, says:

"The capital employed in purchasing in one part of a country in order to sell in another part, the produce of the industry of that country, generally replaces by such operation two distinct capitals that had both been employed in its agriculture or manufactures, and thus enables them to continue that employment.

"The capital used in buying foreign goods for domestic consumption, when the purchase is made by the produce of domestic industry, replaces also two distinct capitals, but *one of them only* supports domestic industry; *the other supports foreign industry,* and therefore foreign trade will give *but one-half the encouragement* to the industry or protective labor of a country that domestic or internal trade does."

We must bear in mind that a nation, whether it buy abroad or produce at home, can have no more than it produces. The development of its home producing power is therefore the only true test of its prosperity, and—Adam Smith being our witness—the importation of articles we can and do make or produce *lessens that development one-half.*

If we can make a roll of cloth, for instance, for $50, and buy it in England for $45, the buyer may gain five dollars, but the nation will really lose $50 which it might use at home, and England will gain that much, and the buyer of the cloth will soon find his ability to purchase decrease, and so will lose in the long run.

We must also bear in mind that there is no discrete degree, no clear line of separation, between producer and consumer. Every producer consumes, every maker is also a buyer; and every consumer produces, or lives on the income of producers. They stand or fall together. Interdependent, their interest is one.

"THE 'BALANCE OF TRADE' THEORY FALLACIOUS—AN EXCESS OF IMPORTS OVER EXPORTS PROOF OF GROWTH IN WEALTH."

A statement like this, for instance, will illustrate the free trade method of showing the fallacy of our export and import reports: A cargo of wheat goes out from New York to Liverpool valued at $50,000, and that makes so much in our official statement of exports; but the American owner sells it in England for $60,000, and gains $10,000, which is added wealth to this country, but makes no official show in Government reports. Or he may invest all his $60,000 in woolens to be imported, and that sum increases our report of total imports, showing in the transaction an excess of $10,000 on the import side, but really representing no added debt abroad, but profit on exports instead. Doubtless such transactions sometimes occur and partially with this result, but the drawbacks are serious. A large part of our exports are bought here by foreigners or their agents, and the profits go to them. Had the supposed American cargo of wheat been exchanged for domestic woolens, all the gains would have remained at home; but in the supposed case, the foreign maker of woolens gets his profits there, and pays his costs of making, wages, &c., there. The goods imported into this country are heavily undervalued in many of our Custom House invoices, on which they pay duty, and really sold at much higher rates; and such undervaluation overbalances the occasional cases like that supposed above. British shipping gets $100,000,000 yearly freight on our exports, to their profit, and that immense profit of theirs—to our loss—makes no show in our official statements. No protectionist would lay an embargo on international trade, but would recognize its use and necessity; but when we find a nation buying more than it sells for any considerable time—that is, with imports greater than exports—that nation is growing poor. The fact that such adverse "balance of trade" is always looked upon with alarm, and spoken of in financial circles with grave apprehension, tells the whole story.

CHAPTER IX.

PROTECTION AND THE FARMERS.

Many farmers are told, and honestly believe, that only the manufacturer has protective duties, while the farm products are open to free trade. The present tariff laws impose the following direct protective duties on agricultural products : Rice cleaned, 2¼ cents per pound ; wheat, 20 cents per bushel ; wheat flour, 20 per cent.; Indian corn, 10 cents per bushel ; oats, 10 cents per bushel ; rye, 10 cents per bushel ; barley, 10 cents per bushel ; butter, 4 cents per pound ; cheese, 4 cents per pound; potatoes, 15 cents per bushel; tobacco, unmanufactured, 35 cents per pound ; sugar, from 1½ to 3½ cents per pound; live animals, 20 per cent.; those for breeding purposes are admitted free to benefit the farmers ; beef and pork, 1 cent per pound ; wool, from 2½ to 10 and 12 cents per pound; and hay, $2.00 per ton. These duties, and others on lesser products, tend to keep out foreign competitors, especially on our northern borders, and leave our home market almost exclusively free for our own farmers.

From 1789 to 1842 an import duty of three cents per pound was placed on cotton, and only removed when utterly useless. It was needed for a time to encourage the growth of that great staple.

The last appeal of the Cobden Club—the Mongredien Western Farmer tract, sent over here by car-loads—is like all the rest from that quarter. Its real meaning (which they do not give) is : Let England be the workshop of the Western world, and you our granary. You grow the food and raw material and let us work it up and send the product back to you at our own price, and so get the lion's share of the profits.

On the opening page of this tract we are told, "He (the Western farmer) is heavily taxed to support unprofitable manufactures in the Eastern States," and the charges are rung on *Western* farmer and *Eastern* manufacturer. The large manufactures of the West are ignored. The benefits of the home market are also cast into convenient darkness.

But the farmer is learning that mills and factories at his door are his natural allies. He learned it long ago in the East. Mr. Greeley tells a story that will illustrate this. "A farmer near Canaan, Connecticut, had always opposed protection as enriching the manufacturer at the expense of his own class. In 1842 he contracted for clearing 100 acres of his woodland at $10 per acre and what could be made from the wood. Before the job was finished the tariff of that year was passed, a furnace for making pig iron from charcoal was put up in his neighborhood, and its owners paid him $20 per acre for the wood on two hundred acres of like woodland. Here was a difference of $6,000 to him between iron made at home and imported (and a home market for all he raised, from cabbages to cattle, besides) The country is thickly dotted with cases like this."

In 1858 the yearly *profit* of British cotton manufactures was estimated at $188,000,000, and the *total value* of our cotton crop at $184,000,000.

Every cotton mill in the South keeps a part of that profit at home, saves transportation, pays better prices for cotton and opens new markets for other farm products which should alternate the cotton crops in the fields around the factory.

SELLING CHEAP AND BUYING DEAR—OLD TIME EXPERIENCES.

Before manufactures were fairly established in this country,—in those days when Andrew Jackson asked: "Where shall the American farmer find a home market for his products?" our farmers were in poor condition indeed, selling cheap and buying dear as compared to their present situation.

An Ohio pioneer once told me of hauling his wheat forty miles to Cleveland, selling it at forty cents a bushel, and buying salt to haul home at five dollars a barrel, and of selling their butter at five cents per pound to buy tea at one dollar fifty cents, and calico at thirty cents a yard.

Mr. Ewing, of Ohio, in a speech in the United States Senate in February, 1832, made this graphic statement:

"Every farmer in Ohio long knew and felt the pressure. Year after year their stacks of wheat stood unthreshed; so low was it reduced, in comparison with manufactured articles, that I have known forty bushels of wheat given for a pair of boots; such was the state of things in the Western country prior to, and at the time of, the revision of the tariff in 1824."

In a speech at Great Falls, New Hampshire, February 21, 1872, by Henry Wilson, afterwards Vice-President of the United States, he said:

"The first month I worked after I was twenty-one years of age, I went into the woods, drove team, cut mill-logs and wood, rose in the morning before daylight and worked hard until after dark at night, and I received for it the magnificent sum of six dollars. Each of those dollars looked as large to me as the moon looked to-night.

"On the farm on which I served an apprenticeship I have seen the best men who ever put scythe in grass working for from fifty to seventy cents a day in the longest days of summer. Yesterday I visited that farm. I asked the men who were there what they paid men in haying-time last summer, and they said from two dollars to two and a half a day. This was paid on the same ground where men worked forty years ago for from fifty cents to four shillings, and took their pay in farm products, not money. I have seen some of the brightest women go into the farm houses and work for from fifty to seventy-five cents a week, milking the cows, making butter and cheese, washing, spinning, and weaving—doing all kinds of hard work. I was told yesterday that many young women were earning in the shops a dollar a day, and that those who worked in houses were getting from two dollars and a half a week to three dollars and a half."

The building up of home manufactures and of railroads necessary for the factories and mills, has lifted the American farmer out of this poor condition, and he is better off than the tiller of the soil in any other country.

WISE INDUSTRIAL POLICY NEEDED FOR SUCCESS IN FARMING.

Our breadth of rich soil, the new wealth of precious metals, and the superior skill and industry of our people doubtless helped this great change; but a wise national industrial policy was an important element, without which it would never have been made. Soil and climate were the same in those days of the poverty of our farmers as now. I can well remember the plain and careful living of the New England farmers in my youth, and now see their children still industrious and thrifty like their parents, but able to live and to dress in a style that would have astonished those worthy ancestors.

My mother used to tell how her father, a farmer in Massachusetts, had the only chaise in town, and how they rode to meeting on Sundays proudly pre-eminent among the plain wagons of their neighbors. Around that same country meeting-house, on a Sunday now, can be seen scores of fine carriages; and the change in dress is as marked as that in these conveyances.

Turkey has an ample space of fine land, and a climate favorable to good farming, Cuba has a soil of wonderful fertility; yet the people of both these countries are miserable.

The union of Ireland with England, by admitting English goods free of tariffs, broke down Irish manufactures, turned her people into poor farmers, brought on the potato rot, and famine swept down over two millions of her population.

A century ago not only did the native hand-looms of Hindostan weave the finest cottons and woolens or cashmeres, but the richest silks, such as for centuries had been carried across the deserts of Central Asia on camels to Europe. But free trade was carried into India at the point of England's bayonets, and with it came the destruction of manufactures, and the turning out of employment of millions of laborers. Theoretically they were free to buy in the cheapest market and sell in the dearest; but, in fact, they could sell nothing and buy nothing. Weavers could not sell their cloths because the English undersold them. The English would not allow their machinery to go to India. Those who made their cloths in England did not buy their crops. Hence the poor Hindoos had no resource but to starve and die by millions, by the roadsides and in the fields. Famines prevailed periodically, as many as two millions of persons dying in a single year.

These countries have rich soil and fine climate, but a

bad industrial policy has wrought sore disaster in their midst. Hindostan is now a part and province of the British Empire, and asks for a protective tariff to guard herself against English monopoly of her manufactures. but asks in vain.

RICH LAND EXHAUSTED.

For forty years the rich valley of the Wabash, in western Indiana, exported its great corn crops to New Orleans,—took all from the soil and put nothing back. That soil seemed inexhaustible, and yielded its eighty bushels per acre; but its decay came. A few years ago a large land owner told me that his average product had come down to thirty-five bushels.

Build the factory near the farm and a large share of what is taken away can be put back.

FARM AND FACTORY NEIGHBORS AND ALLIES.

The following table (from official reports) shows the benefit of making farm and factory neighbors:

	Average product per acre. Bushels.		Cash Value of principal crops per acre.
	Corn.	Wheat.	
Six New England States	35	15.2	$16 52
Ohio	37.5	17 5	16 60
Indiana	29	16.8	13 82
Michigan	40.7	17	16 96
Average of these three Western manufacturing and farming States	35.6	17	15 79
Iowa	38	10.4	9 34
Minnesota	35	13.2	11 54
Kansas	29.3	10	7 98
Average of these three farming States, with fewer factories	34	11 2	9 62
Pennsylvania	40 6	15	$17 33

Of course the area of tillable land is much larger in the West than in New England, but some Western farmers will be surprised to find the grain products per acre in the East larger than in Iowa. The cash value is still more in favor of the States, East and West, where manufactures are most widely spread. Michigan leads the West in products and value, and her home market is large among lumbermen and miners.

Pennsylvania leads all, and this because she has a broad extent of good farming lands with great mills and factories near at hand.

The lesson is plain. WE CANNOT HAVE THE BEST FARMING UNTIL WE HAVE THE BEST MANUFACTURING BESIDE THE FARM.

Dr. Peter Collier, the able chemist of the Agricultural Department at Washington, publishes a table of average crops of corn, wheat, potatoes and hay in 31 States for 1862-70 and for 1871-80, and other facts to make his statement more clear. He concludes that, on the whole; there has been a decrease of productiveness in the last 20 years, and that the increase has been in regions where fertilizers are most used,—in New England and the Middle States. In this older part of our country, where land has been long cultivated, farms yield larger crops than in the West, and their yield improves. *These farms are near the best and most varied manufactures.*

FARM WAGES HERE AND IN ENGLAND.

The Department of Agriculture at Washington has issued a report on the wages of farm labor, from which an extract plainly shows the larger wages and wealth of farmers in manufacturing regions. Those more distant share these benefits, but in less degree:

"The influence of manufactures upon agriculture is seen in the wages of farm labor as well as in the prices of farm production. The rate is higher in Massachusetts than in any other State east of the Rocky Mountains. It is seen in the West as well, affecting the averages of States lying side by side. Ohio has become a manufacturing state of considerable importance. It is dotted over with cities of 20,000 to 60,000 people, largely interested in manufacturing industry. Kentucky, on the other bank of the Ohio, is occupied mainly with the pursuits of agriculture. This fact, together with the larger proportion of negro labor, reduces the rate of wages. The comparison (in 1882) is as follows: Ohio $24.55 per month and Kentucky $18.20.

"In population, variety of industry, and general industrial advancement the northern district of Illinois surpasses the southern. Naturally the wages of agricultural labor reflect this difference. Dividing the State on the line of counties reaching below the 41st parallel, and again on the line of the 29th parallel, the average wages are respectively, from north to south, as follows:

	Per month.
Northern district...	$27 52
Central district...	24 05
Southern district...	19 87

* * * * * * * * *

"Whenever other industries flourish, and the number of persons employed in agriculture is fewer than those engaged in other occupations, it is found that the prices of farm products are also higher in manufacturing districts, and the gross and net earnings of the farm proprietor greater."

The Mark Lane Express (England) has a tabular statement of wages of farm laborers in England and Wales. From sixty-seven districts the range is from $125 to $270 per year—without board. In one case it reaches $295. Sometimes there are perquisites of beer or milk, coal or a cottage at low rent, all from a few shilling up to a few dollars. The average gross income of the English farm hand, as these statements make it, would not be over $180 per year, with which to board and clothe himself and his family. Our farmers—"robbed by protected monopolists"—pay from $200 to $250 per year and board, for like labor; and pay most where these robbers are most plenty—in Massachusetts, for instance.

PURCHASING POWER OF THE FARMER—A COMPARISON.

The average prices of seven leading farm-products, and of seven leading manufactured articles on the imports of which duties are levied, for five free trade or revenue tariff years, and for five protective tariff years are given in the following tables, prepared by Hon. Jonathan Chase, M. C., of Rhode Island. He took his prices from a report of Hon. Mr. Burchard, of Illinois (a free trader), from the *New York Journal of Commerce* (free trade), and from the Philadelphia prices current of iron:

"Let us see what the farmer's articles would buy in the market:

TABLE No. 1.

Articles.	Average prices in five Free Trade years ending in 1850.	Average prices in five Protective Tariff years ending in 1880.
Wheat, bush.	$1 22.8	$1 30.2
Corn, bush.	64.4	52.9
Oats, bush.	42.3	38.72
Butter, lb.	15	24.68
Kentucky tobacco, lb.	5.82	8.48
Wool, lb.	35.58	44.74
Cheese, lb.	6.3	9.04
Coal, ton	5 63	3 62.3
Liverpool salt, sack	1 34.8	72.22
Bleached Sheeting, yard	14.43	11.78
Prints, yard	10.05	7.05
No. 1 pig-iron, ton	25 63	21 75
Refined bar-iron, ton	76 82	50 82
Railroad iron, ton	58 27	40 15

Table No. 2.

	Salt.	Coal.	Bleached sheeting.	Prints.	Pig-Iron.	Bar-iron.	Railroad Iron.
	Sacks.	*Lbs.*	*Yds.*	*Yds.*	*Lbs.*	*Lbs.*	*Lbs.*
One bushel of wheat would buy—							
Under Free Trade	.91	422	8.51	12.21	107.3	35.8	47.23
Under Protection	1.80	719	11.04	16.27	134.00	57.35	72.6
One bushel of corn would buy—							
Under Free Trade	.47	256.	4.46	6.4	56.24	18.78	24.76
Under Protection	.73	328.	4.49	6.65	54.49	23.32	29.55
One bushel of oats would buy—							
Under Free Trade	.31	168.	2.93	4.20	36.94	12.33	16.26
Under Protection	.536	240.	3.27	4.89	39.87	17.07	21.63
Ten pounds of butter would buy—							
Under Free Trade	1.112	597.	10.39	14.92	131	43.74	57.69
Under Protection	3.417	1530	20.95	31.04	254	108.82	137.87
Ten pounds of cheese would buy—							
Under Free Trade	.474	250.	4.36	6.28	55.02	18.37	24.23
Under Protection	1.376	619	8.43	12.52	102.36	43.82	50.53
One pound of wool would buy—							
Under Free Trade	.264	141.	2.46	3.54	31.06	10.37	13.68
Under Protection	.661	296.	4.05	6.00	49.16	21.64	21.08
Ten pounds of Kentucky tobacco would buy—							
Under Free Trade	.431	231.	4.03	5.79	50.82	16.97	22.34
Under Protection	1.117	526.	7.19	10.66	87.33	37.38	47.87

"While the price of corn is comparatively lower than that of any agricultural product, still the farmer can produce it relatively cheaper, and he can land it cheaper at tide-water market.

"But let me proceed with the table: Under free trade the farmer could buy with one bushel of wheat .91 of a sack of Liverpool salt; under protection it would buy 1.8 sacks. Under free trade the bushel of wheat would buy 8.51 yards of bleached sheeting; under protection 11.04 yards. Under free trade it would buy 422 pounds of coal; and under protection 719 pounds. Under free trade it would buy 12.21 yards of prints; under protection 16.27 yards. Under free trade it would buy 107.3 pounds of pig-iron; under protection 134 pounds. Under free trade, 35.8 pounds of bar-iron; and under protection 57.35. Under free trade it would buy 47.23 pounds of railroad iron; under protection 72.6 pounds.

CHEAP TRANSPORTATION.

The total product of iron and steel of all kinds in the Western States in 1880 was 1,912,689 tons, valued at $76,933,686. (See U. S. census.) This required the transportation of 8,000,000 tons of raw materials—ore, coal, limestone, etc.—equal in weight to 264,000,000 bushels of wheat, or three-fourths of the total crop of those States. The more freight the lower rates of transportation, by rail and water. The census reports the freights on wheat from Chicago to New York, all rail the whole year, at $42\tfrac{1}{4}$ cents per bushel in 1868, and $19\tfrac{1}{4}$ cents in 1880, and a corresponding reduction by rail and water.

The *Pall Mall Gazette*, in London, tells the English people that railroad freights are lower per mile in this country than in England, and that they have fallen 45 to 60 per cent. from 1868 to 1878. Mr. H. V. Poor, the great railroad authority, stated to the Bureau of Statistics at Washington that in 1860 the working man in New York City paid $1.60 for the freight of his barrel of flour from Chicago, in 1880 he paid only 86 cents. Edward Atkinson, of Boston, shows that the freight from Chicago to Boston of grain and meat for a year's food for a man costs but $1.25, or a day's work. Thirteen leading railroads, most of them in the West, reduced their charge per ton per mile, from $1\tfrac{77}{100}$ cents in 1873 to $1\tfrac{7}{100}$ cents in 1880, or 38 per cent. For these reductions there are two leading causes,—the larger manufacture of rails at home, and in the West especially;

the immense addition to grain freights of freight of these millions of tons of material for iron and other manufactures.

The annual report of the Milwaukee and St. Paul railway shows that in the 17 years since 1865 the average rate per ton per mile for freight over its line has been reduced from 4.11 cents to 1.70 cents. Competition and improved facilities have made the reduction without the aid of legislation.

The farmer gets a large share of this benefit. Close these western iron mills and his grain freights would rise; build up manufactures at many points and local freights will fall, as through freights have.

The report of the United States Railroad Commissioner for 1882 says: "The United States enjoys the cheapest railroad transportation in the world."

ADDRESS OF E. B. WARD AT WISCONSIN STATE FAIR.

In 1868 the State Agricultural Society of Wisconsin invited E. B. Ward, of Detroit, Michigan, to give the address at its State Fair at Madison. Mr. Ward was a man of broad views and large experience, who had done much, not only as a manufacturer but as a manager of lands and farms, for Western industry. He seldom spoke to public audiences, and only wrote, with a terse brevity, occasional articles which were widely read. Some extracts from his address will give light on this question :

"It is folly for one class to try to stand alone, or to look upon others with jealousy. We depend on each other. Farms or factories only thrive best when they are near each other, so that they can help each other easier. England has no room for farming, as we have, and while her manufacturing puts great wealth in a few bands, her landless people are poor. Here there is room for homes and farms for an independent people. Here are metals, fuel, food, and raw materials for textile fabrics in abundance.

* * * * * * * * *

"Our distinguished political economist, Henry C. Carey, well known on both continents, and whose masterly writings should be in every home library and in every school, well says :

"'Steadiness and regularity in the returns to agricultural labor grow with increase in the variety of commodities produced in the land. Disease tends to disappear as population increases and a near market is created. The poor Irishman sees his potatoes perish of rot, consequent on the increasing exhaustion of soil; the Portuguese witnesses his hopes destroyed by the vine disease; the American farmer is visited by blight, resulting from taking from the soil the material for the ever-recurring wheat crop. The man who has a market at his door finds blight and insects vanish, and is able to make his crops more certain.'

* * * * * * * * *

"Capital likes good investments and quick returns, yet it can live, and wait, and take advantage of poverty. Labor wants constant and decently paid occupation. Diversified industry is desirable to the capitalist, but far more so, and more necessary to the workman. If I had a million dollars it would need no great wit to go into a region where cash was scarce, because the people were far from market, loan money to farmers, and swallow up their farms, according to law, if not according to gospel, by relentless foreclosure of mortgages. But suppose I invested the million in woolen, or cotton, or iron mills, bought the products of those farms for the workmen, and employed the surplus laborers; there need be no mortgages, but the lands would rise five or ten fold in value.

"I should not be acting as a philanthropist, but simply as a business man, helping others to prosper that I might share in that prosperity.

"Let the blood stagnate or move too slow in the veins and a man is sick—the strong and ready pulsation is health. So with business; it is rapid and easy circulation of money, quick returns, nearness of producer and consumer, demand for labor of all kinds, and sale and interchange of its products, that makes health and brings wealth.

"Wherever a large center of consumption is formed, the neighboring farmers are the first to profit by it. This law is infallible, and allows of no exception.

"Shall the hum of the spindle, the roar of the waterfall, the puff of the engine, and the clang of the triphammer cease in your borders, that England may find market for her wares, while you keep on being 'the world's granary' until your land is too poor to raise wheat?

"Agriculture and manufactures are the creators of useful materials and finished products. Commerce only transports and exchanges what they bring into being. Neither can thrive without the other, and neither can gain by overreaching the other.

* * * * * * * * *

"Protection to home industry is the business of a good government, and its advocacy the duty of the intelligent and enlightened citizen. Not monopoly for the benefit of any one class, but protection to that degree needed to encourage manufactures and benefit farmers, and keep our balance of trade healthy. You do not need a tariff on wheat to prevent its import from Europe, for the freight is a tariff; but a roll of English or German cloth is a carload of foreign corn, packed in small compass, and if you buy it you help to keep down the price of your grain to its level.

* * * * * * * * *

"That well-known philanthropist, Peter Cooper, of New York, has carefully prepared a table, from the Treasury Reports of 1856 and 1857, showing the production for each man, woman and child, white or black, in the State, which shows the great advantage of the manufacturing States. I give a part of it to illustrate:

Massachusetts...$166 60
Wisconsin.. 68 41
Rhode Island....................................... 164 61
Indiana.. 99 12
Connecticut....................................... 156 05
California (gold included)........................ 149 96

"Move on in Wisconsin and you can overtop Massachusetts, but you must move in that path. You see the 'Yankee notions' of Connecticut are worth more than the gold nuggets of California, and may learn that the iron mines and fleeces in your midst can be made of more value than richest gold beds.

Protection and the Farmers. 113

"I have nothing to say about motives or intentions, but, in fact, the man who advocates and supports what is called 'free trade' is an enemy to our country's good, and especially to the good of the Northwest.

* * * * * * * * *

"I do not feel like a stranger among you. Coming to this Western country forty years ago, in my boyhood and youth I shared the toils and privations of our pioneer life. I have rolled and burnt logs, and plowed and planted, and hoed and harvested, amidst stumps and girdled trees, with the forests all around the clearings.

"I have sailed along the shores of your then new territory, landing at Milwaukee, when a few rude cabins were the pitiful beginnings of what is now a large and beautiful city. I landed flour in a small boat, lying off the mouth of Chicago river, when there was only a few houses, a ruinous warehouse, an old fort, and a miserable so-called hotel, on the open prairie where now rises another great city, and have always been glad of these my toils and trials, since they earned me the privilege of appreciating the laborious life of the pioneer."

COMPARISON AND CONTRAST—THE WESTERN PROTECTIONIST AND THE COBDEN CLUB SPOKESMAN.

These quotations from the address of Mr. Ward give honest facts not capable of refutation, and the frankly spoken opinions of an able Western man, whose interests were identified, in his own mind, with those of the people he addressed. Compare them with the misstatements of the Cobden Club, through Mongredien, their endorsed spokesman, and see which has the true ring. As a means of making this comparison an extract from a review of the Mongredien tract by Hon. Thomas H. Dudley, of Camden, New Jersey, late U. S. consul at Liverpool, may help us. The extract covers but a part, but his review meets and refutes all the rest with equal force. Mr. Dudley opens by addressing the English writer as follows:

"I visited Europe some few weeks ago, and, a day or two before I left, your pamphlet, issued under the auspices of the Cobden Club, and addressed to the Western farmers of America, was placed in my hands. I was aware that great efforts were to be made by the English people to repeal our Tariff system, and in this way break down our manufactures, but I did not suppose that England, or the Cobden Club, would openly make an attempt to control our elections, even to accomplish this object; but it seems I was mistaken, and it is reserved for you to make an open attempt, the first I have seen. It is a bold move on your part, but the stake you are playing for is an important one for England, and I suppose you think the end justifies the means. The first and primary object of your book is to show the farmers in the United States how badly they are treated by their own government; how grossly they are robbed and swindled, and in this way to prepare them or induce them to vote at the elections for certain candidates with the view of redressing these wrongs and grievances, but in reality to break down our manufactures and transfer the business of this country to England.

THE NUMBER OF FARMERS IN THE UNITED STATES MISSTATED.

"I propose to examine your book and compare it with the facts. You state that the census of 1870 shows 5,922,000 persons engaged in agriculture, and you take this for your basis, and assume that from this there must now be not less than seven millions of persons so engaged, 'nearly all of them having wives and children;' and then you ask what are the annual expenditures on all articles of consumption, except food and drink, of each of these 'families,' and you fix the annual expenditures of each at two hundred dollars. You then, after computing the number of persons so engaged to be seven millions, nearly all of whom have families, and assuming two hundred dollars per annum as the amount expended by each of such persons so engaged as have families, proceed and multiply the whole of the seven millions by the two hundred dollars, without making a single exception for those who have no families; charging every man, woman, and child with consuming or using annually two hundred dollars' worth of products, besides their food and drink. Now, by the census of 1870 there were only 2,659,985 farms in the whole country, and very nearly half a million of these were under twenty acres. *According to your calculation there must have been a little less than three farmers with their families running each farm in the United States.* You ought to have mentioned this fact. Our farmers generally think they run their own farms, and it would have been quite as astonishing to them as most of the other things in your book. You found by our census in 1870 there were 5,922,471 persons engaged in agricultural pursuits. Do you not think it would have been just as well for you, and more just to your readers, to have told them that of this number there were 896,968 females, nearly all in the Southern States, and colored women, who in the days of slavery had been compelled to work as field-hands, and that there were 739,164 children under fifteen years of age, not one-tenth of whom, including the women, probably ever earned so much as one hundred dollars in a year, and the average wages of the other nine-tenths probably would not amount to fifty dollars a year? This, of course, would have spoiled your figuring a little, but it would have been more just to your readers.

THE FARMER PROTECTED BY OUR TARIFF.

"Having taken a look at your figures, and seen on what basis you rest your book, we will take another step in its examination

"1. You state that the Western farmer neither receives nor seeks any legislative protection;

"2. That the farmer in America sells in the cheapest and buys in the dearest markets, and for what he raises he gets a lower price and for what he consumes he pays a higher price than the land-tillers get and pay in any other country in the world;

"3. That by reason of our tariff laws the farmers have to pay the manufacturers in Eastern States four hundred millions of dollars every year more than they would have to pay the English people for the same goods if they were permitted to buy them in England and import them free of duty; that for what they now have to pay one hundred and forty dollars they could buy of a Britisher for one hundred dollars, and that this vast sum of money, to wit, four hundred millions of dollars, year after year, is unnecessarily and wantonly thrown away and wasted, without the least benefit to anybody. You make all these statements without reservation or exception, unless it be some sixty millions of dollars which possibly may go to the legitimate purpose of national revenue.

"Are these statements true or are they false?

"Let us examine them, and first that 'the western farmer neither receives nor seeks any legislative protection.' If the farmer receives protection whether he asks for it or not, your statement is untrue. Is it possible that you were so ignorant, or were the facts concealed on purpose to misrepresent and deceive?

"You admit that rice is protected to ninety-three per cent.

"The duty on wheat is twenty cents per bushel, on Indian corn or maize, ten cents, and other grains, dairy products, meats, wool and sugar pay duties when imported.

"These duties were imposed to protect the farmers, those in the west as well as those in the east. There is no interest in the country more thoroughly protected.

"In addition to the direct protection our farmers receive, under our present tariff system, the incidental protection which they receive by the creation of a home market is even greater and far more important. The direct protection keeps off competitors, and the incidental establishes for them a certain, constant, and reliable home market. Leaving out cotton and tobacco, it is found that about ninety-two per cent of the surplus products of the farmers of the United States are consumed at home, and principally by our Eastern manufacturers and those connected with them, while only eight per cent. are sent abroad. These are about the proportions, one year with another. Destroy the manufactures and you destroy this home market; the market destroyed, and where will the farmer sell his surplus? You will answer, in England. My reply is that England will take just what she requires and no more. England never has taken, and never will take, the place of the home market. Hence this home market to our farmers, both East and West, is of the greatest importance.

THE MARKET IN WHICH THE FARMER BUYS WHAT HE CONSUMES.

"Is your assertion, that for what he consumes he pays more than the land-tiller in any other country, true or false?

"'As to food, including breadstuffs, meat, butter, cheese, lard, eggs, poultry, fruits, potatoes, and other vegetables, you seem to concede that they are cheaper here than they are in England, therefore that they cost less, *and you leave them out.* But you take principally manufactured commodities, and you rest your case upon these. You are careful not to mention tea and coffee, both of which are sold cheaper in our country than they are in England, because we impose no revenue duty upon them and you do. You are good enough to give us a list of some of the goods manufactured in the Eastern States which the Western farmer consumes, and for which you assert positively that he pays forty dollars more on a hundred than he could buy them for in England if it was not for our terrible protective tariff. Your contention, in substance, is that these goods are now selling for forty per cent. cheaper in England than similar kinds and quantities can be bought for in the States. Being in England at the time this pamphlet was placed in my hands, and having had some knowledge and experience in your prices and mode of doing business from my residence of eleven years among you, I set myself at work to ascertain the retail price of some of these commodities, in order to compare them with the price at the retail stores in America. I took the retail price because the farmer generally buys at retail stores.

"Of the textile fabrics consumed or used by our farmers, none are so much used as cotton fabrics. For the last five years we have been continuously shipping our cotton goods to England, *but, for your own purposes, you ignore the fact that cotton goods are cheaper in the United States than in England.* If you will put yourself to the trouble to go to your own dry goods stores in England, you will find on their shelves our cotton fabrics for sale, and at prices as cheap as, if not cheaper than, you can manufacture and sell them for. Your statement, then, about the farmer's wife being able to buy a calico dress in England for two dollars, for which she now has to pay three dollars in America, is untrue. And this applies to hosiery as well as to prints and plain cotton goods. It is the same with boots and shoes. If you will take the trouble to examine your own trade returns, printed by order of Parliament, you will find that you have been importing boots and shoes from the United States, and if you will go still farther, and do as I have done, go to your stores in England and then to our stores in this country, you will find that the farmers in the United States can buy their boots and shoes just as cheap here as they can in England.

"If you will then go into your hardware stores you will see displayed for sale, imported from the United States, axes, edge-tools, forks, etc., etc., superior in quality and finish and cheaper than you can make them. This is generally admitted, even in England. The American farmer would be a great loser if he was compelled to go to England for any of his tools or implements of husbandry.

"Furniture constitutes a large item in the expenses of every farmer's family, but you do not mention furniture; was its omission due to the fact that it is about ten per cent. on an average cheaper in the States than it is in England?

"The farmers in America generally have time-pieces. Why did you not refer to them? We furnish most of the clocks found in the houses of the farmers of your own country. Last year you imported from the United States 376,023 clocks. Probably in your next issue you will explain and show how these clocks could be repurchased in England by the Western farmers and brought back to this country so as to save forty per cent. over and above what they would have cost if they had bought them here. Pots, pans, kettles, and tinware of all kinds are retailed as cheap here as in England, and so with our pressed glassware.

"So much for the markets in which the farmer buys what he consumes, and the prices he has to pay. We have seen that your statements in this are about like those in the other instances."

The comparison needs no comment. Will you pay heed to the English free trader or to the American protectionist in Wisconsin?

GRAIN AND PROVISIONS—EXPORTS AND HOME CONSUMPTION.

Our production of grain, and our exports of wheat have increased largely. In 1881 our home consumption of wheat was 295,962,780 bushels, and our exports 184,886,943 bushels. Corn, a larger and more valuable crop than wheat, is much less exported. In 1880 but 88,000,000 bushels were sent abroad, while 1,629,434,543 bushels were used at home. Short crops in Europe and large yields at home made our wheat exports very large, but these favoring conditions are not permanent.

In the last thirty years there has been a surprising growth in the magnitude of the production and trade of the world, and especially of our own country. New implements have helped the farmer to till and harvest great crops; new machinery and new processes have increased manufactured products; we have built railways through vast regions of productive lands and welcomed hosts of industrious emigrants to till those fields, and the abundance of the precious metals has stimulated this development, while our protective policy has made it sure.

Late census statistics give the United states 4,008,907 farms in 1880, an increase from 2,659,985 in 1870 which does not show any ruin to farmers.

A writer in the New York *Herald* finds the prices of farm products stated in a newspaper in the interior of that State in 1816, and compares them with 1882 as follows:

Products.	1816.	1882.
Wheat	25c. to 44c.	$1.42
Corn	12½c. to 20c.	.60
Oats	15c.	.60
Eggs, per dozen	5c.	.15
Barley, per bushel	25c.	.80
Butter, per pound	5c. to 12c.	.40
Cheese, per pound	3c. to 6c.	.13
Cows, per head	$16 to $20	$20 to $100
Cattle, per yoke	$25 to $45	$100 to $250
Hay, per ton	$3 to $5	$10 to $20
Straw, per ton	$2 to $4	$7 to $16
Carriage horses, per span	$150 to $200	$500 to $1,200
Sheep, per head	50c. to 75c.	$1.50 to $2.50
Farm labor, per month	$3 to $8	$12 to $25.

The following prices (from the *Boston Journal*) in 1816 and 1882 for a few manufactured goods and other merchandise purchased by the farmer indicate the great change in favor of the agricultural classes and other consumers during the interval :

ARTICLES.	1816.	1882.
Steel, per pound.............................	17c.	10c.
Sawplate, per pound........................	40c.	26c.
Nails, per pound.............................	12½c.	4c.
Broadcloth, per yard........................	$16.	$4
Wool blankets, per pair....................	$10 to $20	$3 to $10
Cotton cloth, per yard......................	30c. to 50c.	4c. to 12c.
Calico, per yard...............................	25c. to 75c.	4c. to 16c.
Salt, per bushel..............................	$1 to $4	15c. to 25c.

That is to say, the average increase in the price of farm produce during the last sixty-six years has been from 300 to 400 per cent., while the average decrease of the price of manufactured goods during the same period has been from 20 to 90 per cent.

While our foreign market has grown, we must keep clearly in mind the immense importance of our home consumption—more stable and larger.

Dr. G. B. Loring, U. S. Commissioner of Agriculture, said in New York in November, 1881:

"The aggregate annual product of the manufacturing and mechanical industries of the United States is now about $6,000,000,000. Of this, less than $200,000,000 are exported. And of the $9,000,000,000 produced by agriculture, *less than ten per cent. is exported.* * * * * *

"I have alluded to the producing power of the American people, but in order to understand the relations which exist between our industries we should not forget our consuming capacity also. Of the $15,000,000,000 produced by our various industries nearly

$14,000,000,000 are consumed at home. It is the home market to which the American producer turns most naturally, let his industry be what it may."

This shows our home trade and consumption *fourteen times greater than our large foreign trade.* He goes on to show the value of fruits and other perishable crops, sold only in near markets, lost when the farm is far from the factory or the town, and worth many millions.

PROVISIONS—EXPORTS.

Only our grain crops have been considered, but the same economic laws apply to the other products of the farm. For all these our exports are large, but the home demand much larger and better. Leaving out cotton and tobacco, and it is estimated that *but eight per cent. of our farm products are exported,* and ninety-two per cent. consumed at home. By a late report of the Bureau of Statistics at Washington, our exports of provisions, other than breadstuffs, in 1881 were $143,723,663, of which Great Britain took over $100,000,000. To get even five per cent. reduction in the prices of our farm products would be a yearly gain to England of $25,000,000, and a free trade agitation, even if it does not change our tariff legislation, checks our manufactures, pushes more surplus grain and provisions abroad at lower rates, and is a snug way for our British cousins to get that sum, or more, *our farmers being the losers.*

A HEALTHY EQUILIBRIUM.

It is a sound principle in political economy that the manufactures and the agriculture of a country should be developed in healthy equilibrium to each other, that each may supply the wants of the other, each improve the other, and the country be self-dependent. Plainly enough, the non-agricultural industries of the United States must move on with strong and rapid steps to keep pace with the agricultural.

England has no room for farms to feed her factories; we have too few factories for our farms, but room enough for both, and so we can reach that equilibrium which she cannot attain for want of room. To reach it is the aim and idea of a protective policy. To destroy it—to make the western farmer send his grain and meat to feed the Leeds factory hand in England, and buy the cloth he weaves after it has been sent across ocean and mountain and prairie—is the aim of British free trade.

In a Congressional speech January 27th, 1883, Hon. D. C. Haskell, M. C., of Kansas, stated this case very clearly:

"In 1840 the number of persons engaged in agriculture was 3,717,536; in 1880 the number was 7,670,493; population of the United States in 1840, 17,069,453; population of the United States in 1880, 50,155,783.

"It will be seen that from 1840 to 1880 the number of persons engaged in agriculture had a little more than doubled, while the total population of the United States from 1840 to 1880 had nearly trebled.

"In other words, in 1840 each farmer had of neighbors, non-producers of agricultural products, to buy his produce, 4⅖ persons; in 1880 he had 6¼ persons who were consumers of his products, an enormous increase in demand of nearly 50 per cent. Had the nation been remanded to the productions of agriculture for support to the same extent as it was in 1840, and had the number of farmers increased as the total population increased, there would now be in the United States 3,000,000 more persons engaged in agriculture than there are.

"The farming interest of to-day has in the United States of consumers, non-producers of agricultural products, not competitors with it, a population of nearly seventeen millions more than it would have had had the ratio of producers and consumers of 1840 been continued.

"Will any one, in the light of these facts, sneer at this "home market" of seventeen millions? The statesmen of the past saw in their day farmers' produce, under free trade policy, unsalable at any price. We see a steady demand at living prices for anything and everything edible that the farmer can produce, while the prices of all manufactured articles tend lower and lower year by year."

Mr. G. B. Dixwell well says (review of Perry's "Farmers and the Tariff"): "In twenty-five years the population of our whole country will be doubled; that of the now less settled portions increased three to five fold. Let the farmer consider whether he would prefer the increase to be mostly farmers, or people who buy and do not produce farm products. It will not take him long to make up his mind; and his judgment will be worth as much as that of all the political economists of Europe and America. His judgment will agree with the mature and deliberate opinion of such men as Franklin, Hamilton, Jefferson, Andrew Jackson, Henry Clay, Webster, and the majority of the great statesmen who have been the pride of our country."

UNCERTAINTY OF THE FOREIGN MARKET.

Hon. J. R. Dodge, statistician of the United States Agricultural Department at Washington, said in one of his reports:

"There is no doubt that the wheat farmer is at the *mercy of the foreign demand*. If British fields are blighted, there is rejoicing on our prairies over remunerative harvests. If the garners of Continental Europe are full and England's wants at a minimum, there is dissatisfaction at the West, liable to be ventilated on the currency, the tariff or the railroads. * * The heaviest foreign demand may occur in a season of low production, and the lightest in a year of abundance, increasing the fluctuation. * * * The wheat-grower is at one time elated with remunerative prices, and at another depressed by rates which fail to pay the cost of production. The grain crop of 1878, for instance, larger by six per cent. in quantity than that of 1877, was less in value by twenty-one per cent.

"The exports of breadstuffs in eight months, up to February, 1881, were $47,000,000 less than in the same time a year before. Wheat fell off 35,000,000 bushels."

It may be said that our home market is not free from troublesome fluctuations. This is true, but they are less than those abroad; because the home market depends mainly on our own crops and welfare, while the markets abroad depend on the crops and welfare of several countries.

The Michigan farmer, near the lumber regions, sells his hay, wheat, oats, and corn, to the camps and mills at good rates, largely independent of foreign prices-current. The Pennsylvanian, with a sale for his produce at the great iron mill near by, is less troubled about trans-Atlantic ups and downs than his brother husbandman in Iowa. The more factories everywhere near the farms the more this independence becomes national. Having a surplus to export, as the Western farmer has and will have, it is natural and wise that he should watch distant marts and seek cheap transportation; but it is far from natural or wise for him to be jealous of home manufactures, or in favor of a free trade policy to injure them.

"HOW PROTECTION PROTECTS FARMERS."

Such is the title of a paper read by Mr. Dodge at a meeting of the Association of American Economists, in Washington, D. C., February 15th, 1883, reported as follows:

"Protection enhances the value of land. The theory is that withdrawal of labor from agriculture to manufactures and mining increases production, stimulates improvements, compels higher culture and soil fertilization, and makes land more productive, and hence more valuable. This is also fact as well as theory, that is patent to everybody and defies disproval. The census returns are a repository of millions of such facts. Virginia is a great State in advance of Pennsylvania in settlement, and for a long period, in population. It is rich in agricultural resources, in coal and iron, water power, wood, and timber. So is Pennsylvania. The former is essentially an agricultural State, though destined to become great in mining and manufacturing. It had in 1880, according to the census, 51.41 per cent. of her people in agricultural occupations. The value of her farm land was $10.89. Pennsylvania had but 20.68 per cent. of her workers employed in agriculture, and her farm lands were worth $49.30 per acre. So with other States. Ohio has 40 per cent. of her people engaged in farming, and her farm lands average $45.97. Kentucky, across the river from Ohio, nearly 62 per cent., and her lands, some of which are the finest in the world, are worth only $13.92 per acre. Two other States, lying side by side on the same parallel, settled by people of similar origin and equal intelligence— Illinois and Iowa—the former has a little over 43 per cent. in agriculture and lands valued at $31.87 per acre, the latter over 57 per cent. and lands worth $22.92. So it is elsewhere and everywhere. A state or nation with little productive industry except the cultivation of the soil has little wealth, few markets, and no inducement to produce a surplus of anything. Protection increases the value of production. * * * Dividing the States and Territories into four sections, the first comprising the manufacturing and mining areas, and including all having a smaller proportion than 30 per cent. of the occupied population of the working class engaged in agricultural employments; the second section comprising States having more than 30 and under 50 per cent.; the third including all having over 50 per cent. and less than 70 per cent., and the fourth including all States with more than 75 per cent. engaged in farming, we have the following perfectly natural, not to say inevitable, results: First section, average value of product per man, $467; second section, $394; third, $261; fourth, $161. Thus the States with less than 30 per cent. of their people engaged in farming realize nearly three times as much per man as those which have over 70 per cent. in farm work. In other words, one man in the first section realizes as much as three men in the last."

The British Royal Agricultural Commission Report in 1882 said: "It is safe to say that, for the last two years, the agriculture of America has been at the very flood tide of its prosperity." Their statement confirms the views of Mr. Dodge.

A FARMER'S STATEMENT.

In a late speech in Congress, Hon. J. T. Updegraff, M. C., an Ohio farmer, put the case as follows:

"I have been a farmer all my life, and every year for thirty years have sold the products of the farm. When manufactures were fully protected and flourishing, I have never seen the time that judicious agriculture was not prosperous; and when manufacturing under "revenue" tariff was crippled or broken down I never saw agriculture flourishing. Sometimes a certain product may be in demand temporarily, but the uniform rule is as I have stated it. If any member has seen it otherwise, let him declare it. [Applause.] No; the real and permanent industries of a people are always in harmony and interdependence with each other. Each member of a community profits by an increase in the productive power of the whole body. That advantage is increased and multiplied by every increase in the diversity of employments. The farming interest above every other is benefited by this diversity, which saves the necessity of carrying bulky products to a distant market; for every intelligent farmer knows that the man who is compelled to go to market must, in some way, pay the cost of going, and that the very first of all the charges paid, by labor or by land, is that for transportation."

THE WOOL TARIFF—GARFIELD'S REPORT.

The tariff on wool and woolens (somewhat modified by Congress last winter) was perfected in 1867, by mutual consultation between growers and manufacturers leading to congressional legislation. Its results, as to wool, are given in the Tariff Commission Report, and can be stated as follows: Sheep in 1860, 22,471,-275; in 1880, 43,576,897. Pounds of wool in 1860, 60,264,913; in 1880, 240,000,000—*or twice as much per head as in 1860.* Prices in Boston, in currency, averaged, in 1867, 51 cents; in 1875, 43 cents; in 1880, 48 cents. The price a little lower, but *the sum from each fleece nearly double, as the result of improved breeds under protective encouragement and with a home market*—the growers benefited, with no added cost to the consumers.

The last labor, as a Congressman, of James A. Garfield was a report favoring the retention of the duty on wool. It occupied him up to the very hour of leaving his Washington home for Chicago, where he was nominated for President. In that report, May 24th, 1880, he said :

"Should it (the removal or unjust change of the wool tariff) become a law, it will be impossible for our farmers to compete in the market with the mestiza wools of South America; and it will be equally impossible for our manufacturers to compete with those of France and England. Of course, any legislation that destroy the woolen manufacturers is equally destructive to sheep husbandry, for the farmer would no longer have a market for his wool. That nation can hardly be called independent which does not possess the materials and the skill to clothe its own people.

* * * * * *

"In 1860 we were largely dependent for our clothing upon foreign wool growers and foreign manufacturers, at such prices as they were able to dictate. Now, the woolen fabrics used by our people are mainly manufactured by the skill and labor of our own artisans from the product of our own flocks. No attentive observer who visited the Centennial Exposition failed to notice the astonishment with which the French and English manufacturers examined the fine cloths produced by American looms; and no feature of that great exhibition reflected more credit upon American enterprise and skill.

* * * * * *

"As a revenue measure, the tariff of 1867 on wools and woolens has been very effective, having produced $360,000,000 of revenue in the last thirteen years, an average of $28,000,000 per annum."

INCREASE OF FARMING WEALTH 1860 TO 1880.

Edward Young, late chief of the United States Bureau of Statistics, gives the following facts, telling the growth of farming wealth in twenty years of a protective tariff—a growth unequalled, and the more wonderful when we think of the awful waste of a great civil war during this period.

These eloquent figures need no comment.

SUBJECTS.	1860.	1880.	Increase, per cent.
Value of farms...............	$3,271,575,426	$10,197,161,905	212
Wheat produced, bushels.....	173,104,924	498,549,868	188
Wheat exported, "	4,155,153	153,252,795	3,603
Corn produced, ".	838,792,742	1,717,434,543	105
Corn exported, "	3,314,305	98,169,877	2,862
Wool produced, pounds.......	60,264,913	232,500,000	286
Cotton produced, bales........	3,826,086	6,343,269	65
Oats produced, bushels........	172,043,185	407,858,999	136
Barley produced, "	15,825,898	44,113,495	179
Cheese exported, pounds......	15,524,830	127,553,907	722
Hogs packed..................	2,350,822	6,950,451	196
Improved lands, acres.........	163,110,720	287,211,845	76

Official figures give like facts as follows:

VALUE OF	1860.	1870.	1880.
Farm implements and machinery.	$ 246,000,000	$ 336,878,000	$ 900,000,000
Live stock.......	1,107,500,000	2,447,539,000	5,000,000,000

The peaceful march of an army of skilled and stalwart artisans should be westward, where, as the poet tells us,
 "The star of empire takes its way."
Another like army of occupation should march southward, where room is ample and raw material abundant. Farmers and merchants, and all the people, should wheel into line, and over the united hosts should be flung out a white banner with the golden motto on its broad folds: PROTECTION TO HOME INDUSTRY—THE AMERICAN MARKET FOR THE AMERICAN PEOPLE.

CHAPTER X.

WAGES AND PROTECTION.

Low wages means coarse and scanty living, defective education, narrow thought and cramped life. Beautiful virtue and spiritual grace sometimes light up the homes of the poor, but large populations standing on the verge of want are not the nurseries of the best manhood and womanhood. On the broad scale hard work at pauper pay makes human life dull and sickly, or breeds passion and crime. Inevitably, too, such a condition creates a jealous hatred toward those who win wealth from ill-paid toil. The noblest aspirations and hopes are crushed, and there comes a weight of dumb despair or a mood of bitter endurance.

Gerald Massey, son of a poor English working man, knew the feelings of the class from whence he sprang, and could utter them in impassioned words. He said:

"Press on! A million pauper-foreheads bend in misery's dust;
God's champions of the golden truth still eat the mouldy crust:
This damning curse of tyrants must not kill the nation's heart;
The spirit in a million slaves doth pant on fire to start,
And strive to mend the world, and walk in Freedom's march sublime;
While myriads sink heart-broken, and the land o'er-swarms with crime.
'Oh God!' they cry, 'we die, we die, and see no earnest won!'
Brothers, join hand and heart, and in the work press on!"

Such wages as give possibility for comfort and taste, for accumulation, education, and the hope of a larger life, tend to good feeling and to harmony and equality of rights and condition. The fairly paid artisan or laborer feels less a slave and more a co-operative helper of the employer, with common hopes and interests. He is *a man* and not a human machine.

Our protective policy is of more value to the workman than to the capitalist,—is indeed largely a matter of wages. Our duties on imports are no more than equivalents for the larger pay of the American workman. With labor as cheap as in England we could produce cheaper here than there.

In his report on iron and steel, as U. S. Commissioner to the Paris Exposition in 1867, Abram S. Hewitt said:

"We have seen that the cost of making iron in England, Belgium and France varies from $32.50 to $40 per ton, and $5 additional pays its transportation to our seaboard ports. At these same ports American iron cannot be delivered at less than $60 in gold, against $40 for the foreign article, and *the entire difference consists in the higher wages, and not in the larger quantity of labor required for its production in the United States*, where the physical, mental and moral condition of the working classes occupy a different standard from their European *confreres*, and where wages cannot be reduced without violating our sense of the just demands of human nature."

Such reduction of wages in this country, fortunately, is not possible, certainly is far from desirable, and is not wished for by a large majority of employers. They know and feel that the conditions of trade and production which enable them to pay our present rates are better for all.

Free trade for the United States means low wages. In his address at the Wisconsin State Fair, E. B. Ward said :

"The elevation of labor is called 'the sentiment which created civilization.' Sometimes we find a frank statement of the effects of free trade, as in a late New York journal, where a writer says: 'I am for unqualified free trade. I would sell out the Custom Houses, discharge the leeches there, and allow people to sell and buy wherever they please. This will bring us to a true and normal relation. Commercial disturbance would result. We should be on a new foundation. The first effect would be to stop manufacturing here and fill the country with foreign goods, many of which Europe would never see her money for. A commercial revolution would follow, laborers would be out of employment, *and the price of labor would come down, down, until it reached the European standard, and then success is assured.*' Success, possibly, for the few, but hard work at pauper pay for the many!"

The *Chicago Western Manufacturer* finds in the Cincinnati *Trade List* the statement that a well-known Kentucky free trader (whose name they will give if called for) said to them a few months ago that low wages was just what he and his associates wanted. He observed: "The laborer in this country is getting to be too smart and independent. Unless he is brought down a peg pretty soon he will rule us all. He gets too much by half. You exclaim against foreign competition, because it will reduce the price of labor. I favor it for exactly the same reason. I want to see these ignorant fellows, who know nothing except to work with their dirty hands, brought down to their proper level. We will never prosper in this country until it is done."

AMERICAN AND FOREIGN WAGES AND EXPENSES.

By a condensation of tables of wages and cost of food,—from State Department, Labor, 1878,—we find the average weekly wages of seventeen trades—bricklayers, blacksmiths, shoemakers, etc.—to be, in England $7.57, Scotland $7.22, New York $12.70, Chicago $11.50. The cost of thirteen kinds of food,—breadstuffs, meat, butter, etc.—is $2.50 in Liverpool, $1.30 in New York, $1.10 in Chicago for a like quantity—a pound of each kind, or thirteen pounds in all. Rent would be somewhat cheaper in Great Britain, but houses much poorer. The whole mode of life there poorer than here, among like classes, and the ability to save from wages less, as will be shown more fully. The British Almanac, 1881, stated that but 59 per cent of Irish laborers ate meat, and those but 5 ounces a week. U. S. Consul Farrell reports from Bristol, England, in 1881, average wages of farm laborers per week, without board $4.00; and the State Department table quoted from gives the same wages for England $3.60, Scotland $4.25.

An English government agent's report, from this country, gives this statement:

"A laboring man with a family of eight children told me the other day, after reviewing with this man in regard to the great saving on the necessaries of life in his native country (Germany), as compared with his adopted country, and asking him how much better off he considered himself by the move, he replied in substance: 'I am ever so much better off. My earnings in Germany (as a plasterer) would be barely 3 shillings a day, while here they are from 11 to 12 shillings. My eldest boy, who is just sixteen years old, makes his 4 shillings a day already, more than I could have done myself at home, and pays me something for his board. Even my youngest, of thirteen, earns 8 shillings a week, while he learns a trade. In Germany neither of the two would bring home a sixpence. In short, if I were there I should, with my large family, be little better than a pauper, while here I have saved enough already to purchase a comfortable cottage, and I have something in the savings bank still.' It is worth noting—

Says the writer—

that in this, as in every similar case which has come within my own personal knowledge, the laborer's cottage has been purchased with savings laid up since 1860."

Our consul at Cologne reports—

Masons, per day	70 cents
Carpenters, per day	50 to 72 "
Engine fitters, per day	71 to 77 "
Blacksmiths, per day	67 to 71 "

The report of the tariff commission gives the following as the wages paid in England and Pittsburg, Pa., for manufacturing iron:

	England.	Pittsburg.
Puddling, per ton	$1 94	$5 50
Shingling, per ton	29	77
Rolling in puddle mill, per ton	29	68¾
Rolling and heating, per ton	1 80	4 80
Common labor	56@72	1 30@150

Mr. Edward Young, former chief of U. S. Bureau of Statistics at Washington, makes the following statement:

Wages in Rolling Mills, 1878.	Middleboro, Eng.	Pennsylvania.
Puddlers	$10 50	$21 15
Top and bottom rollers	16 05	27 50
Rail mill rollers	21 05	40 00
Merchant mill rollers	12 10	36 83
Machinists	8 59	15 56
Engineers	8 47	15 24
Laborers	4 65	8 58
Iron molders	6 77	11 00
Pattern makers	7 01	14 69

Mr. Casson, the general manager of the Earl of Dudley's Staffordshire iron works, in his recent visit to Pittsburgh, in answer to a question by a reporter of the Pittsburgh *Commercial-Gazette*, said:

"I find that in many respects you have the advantage of us as regards mechanical appliances, while in others we are greatly ahead of your manufacturers. We can manufacture iron at just one-half the cost as far as the price of labor is concerned. I find that your rate of wages is about exactly double what we have to pay."

In the face of such testimony as this, a tract issued by the New York Free Trade Club in 1882, entitled "Census Revelations Respecting Wages, &c.," of "Iron and Steel Industries," quotes the statement of James M. Swank, of Philadelphia, iron and steel census taker, that "the wages of labor in this country are much higher than in any other iron-making country in the world," and says: "It is in conflict with all other testimony; we cannot accept it." It also affirms: "But in point of fact, the English wages in this department of industry are not far from the very low rates of wages here, if indeed they are not actually higher." The worthlessness of this tract may be judged by the recklessness of these assertions. The same tract states the average wages of iron and steel workers at $1.30 per day by the census of 1880. Its figures are 140,975 persons employed, with total wages of $55,476,785. Their result appears correct, but is not, for they assume that all these men were employed every day of the three hundred, or three hundred and forty working days of the year. This is not true. Some chose not to work constantly, and others earned money in other ways when not in the mills. This method of making wages appear lower than they are is applied to other industries.

On the contrary, our reports of English wages are sometimes too high. In the Report on Labor, by W. M. Evarts, Secretary of State, quoted by O. S. Hill, of the State Department, as "standard authority," we learn that "the English rates (wages) are more apparent than real, and that while nominally the English workman appears to receive a comparatively high rate of wages, he only works on half or two-thirds time, thus gratifying his desire to preserve a high rate of wages, at the expense of a sentimental fiction which is neither profitable nor substantial."

Along with this effort to make wages appear less than they are is another to make the employer's profits appear too large, and so make out a case against the "protected monopolists."

They take, for instance, the census figures of the iron and steel industry, and this would be the mode of statement:

Value of materials used...............	$191,271,150
Total wages paid.......................	55,476,785
Total cost of product...............	$246,747,935
Value of product.....................	$296,557,385
Deduct cost............................	246,747,935
Profit.................................	$49,809,450

This is 22 per cent. on the capital of $230,971,884 invested, *but insurance, decay and interest are left out.* Does an iron mill, or a woolen mill, last forever? Suppose it to last twenty-five years. The annual loss is four per cent., and all these items which are not counted can be reckoned as twelve per cent. at least, leaving ten per cent. *net* profit instead of twenty-two per cent. This is a good profit in a prosperous year, and helps to make up years in which such mills paid nothing.

It may be said, wages are higher in England than in protective Germany, and this shows that they are not affected by free trade or protection. In old and densely peopled countries, where aristocratic institutions have made life poor and servile among the people, we yet find that where there are large, varied, and well established industries, labor and skill are more employed, and better paid, than in other old countries with fewer and feebler industries. England, *by rigidly protective tariffs*, persistent vigor, and careful attention to her industries for centuries,—an attention that hardly a nation in Europe, certainly not Germany, has given for so long a time— brought her great manufactures to a solid condition, and therefore wages are higher than in Germany. Her short free trade career has not yet broken down this result of her long protective policy, but her wages are much lower than ours. In our new and active country labor is in demand; our manufactures, built up under protection, help greatly to keep up that demand and to hold wages to our higher level, which could not be done under free trade. A protective policy lives, and is to live, in this country, and our intelligent people see that, for them, free trade means poor pay for poor work—the lower level of a European working life.

The Germans, and other Europeans, started with a coarse and narrow life, and have risen in the scale as their industries have grown under a protective policy. That policy works *upward*, but can work no miracles, and is hampered by military conscriptions in Europe, and by other troubles from which we are fortunately free. The German Iron and Steel Association report tabulates the returns from 338 iron and steel makers and machinists, and gives 15 per cent. increase of wages from 1879 to 1882, under their new protective measures.

In this country we started with a higher level of life, and with institutions aiming for personal freedom and equal rights. Our people never have, and never will, accept the pauper pay and hopeless lot of Old World toilers. Facts show plainly enough that protection is a bar against lower wages in this country; that in all countries their industrial policy affects the price of labor, protection helping to better work and pay; and that other influences,—previous condition, race, free or despotic institutions, intelligence, etc.,—have their share in the matter. England had the oldest protective policy, and the best institutions comparatively, and her wages are above those on the Continent. France began her protective policy earlier than Germany, and her wages are higher.

Free traders say that we have no protective tariff against the self-importation of cheap laborers, and that therefore this talk about higher wages is absurd, while foreigners are free to come here and share and reduce them. In our broad land we want emigrants, and they help in needed work and add to our wealth, therefore it would be absurd to hinder their coming. It often takes the slow savings of years for a poor workman to come from Europe to America, and that is barrier enough without a tax on immigration ill suited to the genius of our government. Yet they come largely, to share our better life. The tide sets Westward and the returning tide is but the spray tossed back by the mighty waves sweeping across the Atlantic. How protection crushes the working man! Yet he toils and saves for years to pay his way here to be crushed! Granting that immigration may cheapen labor, it is better for us to feed and clothe the laborer here than to admit the products of his cheap labor free from abroad and send food and money across the ocean to pay for them, as free trade would have us do.

It is said that British workmen are better off under

free trade than they were under protection. The pitiful fact is that the policy of that government, under whatever name, has paid small attention to the condition or wants of the people. Centuries ago laws were enacted regulating wages, but they were framed to compel men to work for certain specified pay rather than to prohibit employers from oppressing the poor.

President Hamlin, of Middlebury College, Vermont, criticising Professor Perry on "The Farmer and the Tariff" in *The American Protectionist* in New York, says of free trade in England:

"It does not diminish pauperism. In England the laboring classes, manufacturing and agricultural, are no better off than they were fifty or one hundred years ago. On the contrary, the difference between them and the rich is greater than ever. If free trade has been a blessing to England, her millions of laborers have no share in it. They have made no progress. The wonderful inventions of the age, the better modes of living, the higher enjoyments of life, pass them by in the sweat and grime of their ill-requited toil; and if hope ever comes to them at all, it is the immortal hope of another life.

"In proof of this assertion that free trade has in no respect benefited the laborers of England, on the farm or in the workshop, I quote from one of the most distinguished advocates of free trade in England—Henry Fawcett, M. P., Professor of Political Economy in the University of Cambridge.

"In his 'Political Economy,' extensively used as a text-book in this country and in England (page 133), after referring to the prodigious increase of British exports, he adds, 'This increase of national prosperity has as yet effected no corresponding improvement in the condition of the laboring classes.' He then goes on to state that where there has been an increase of wages there has been a proportionate increase in the cost of living, so that one barely compensates for the other.

"He then refers to Mr. Brassey, who is another distinguished free-trader. His book on 'Work and Wages' Prof. Fawcett endorses as of the highest authority, as perfectly accurate, as evincing the most careful investigation. The following are some of the results:

"In the Canada Engineering Works at Birkenhead, thirteen different classes of workmen are employed, such as fitters, turners, coppersmiths, etc.; of these thirteen classes six were receiving less wages in 1869 than in 1854, three were receiving the same, and four were receiving somewhat higher wages.

"In one of the Government dockyards, the result was even less favorable. From 1849 to 1859 three classes had an advance of sixpence a day, but from 1859 to 1869 no advance whatever. 'Wages were absolutely stationary throughout these years' (page 134).

"Twenty classes of laborers in private ship-yards on the Thames showed the same wages in 1869 as in 1851. There was a temporary rise in 1865, but it was dearly purchased by the distress that followed.

"Mr. Brassey thinks that building-trades are somewhat better paid, but 'the increase in wages has not been proportionate to the increase in the cost of living.' Prof. Fawcett confesses that 'in other trades the condition of the laborer must have deteriorated' (p. 135). But even in the very best paid trades it must also have deteriorated, according to his own showing.

"It is a point of interest and essential to a right judgment upon free trade in England, to know how great has been the increase in the expenses of living during these years of its greatest development. Prof. Fawcett (p. 134) considers it not less than thirty per cent! The best paid laborers, who are comparatively few, have hardly held their own. What, then, is the condition of the multitude? What has free trade bestowed upon the English laborer in general, on the farm and in the workshop? It is the same as a decrease of wages during the last thirty years of almost one-third. His condition, never very hopeful, is now hopeless."

Robert P. Porter, late member of the Tariff Commission, writes from Leeds, England, a great centre of woolen mills, to the *New York Tribune,* under date of January 23d, 1883, and gives a list of the wages of twenty grades of operatives in those mills, as computed from their account books, and also a like list of wages for the same work in New England mills, from the report of C. D. Wright, Massachusetts labor statistician. The English wages range from $7.50 to $2.50 (for boys), and average $4.65 per week; the American wages range from $13.43 to $4.81, and average $7.79 per week. Hon. W. A. Russell, M. C., makes a like comparison of nineteen grades of worsted mill operatives in both countries, from reports of treasurers here and authentic documents there, and makes English weekly wages average $7.94 for 56 hours' work per week, and American pay average $16.73 for 60 hours' work.

Hours of labor and currency at or below par are to be thought of. For instance, wages in some years between 1860 and 1870 were in depreciated currency, and appear more than they were. These items cannot always be exactly estimated, but the best authorities giving nearest to accurate facts, are quoted.

Professor Leone Levi, of London, in his "Estimates of the Earnings of the Working Classes," gives the average earnings of 551 workers in an English cotton mill at $3.56 per week in 1867. In April, 1869, the wages of 2,997 Pacific Mill operatives, a woolen mill at Lawrence, Massachusetts (their whole force), averaged $7.83 (or $5.87 in gold) per week, a difference of $2.31 gold, or 65 per cent., in favor of the American mills. The excess of wages above cost of board and lodging was somewhat greater in our favor. Of 781 housekeepers in the Pacific mills, Mr. Greeley says (see Political Economy) that 227 lived in their own houses, worth $413,163, or an average of $1,820 to each family, mostly their own earnings. This comparison might be even more favorable to-day, as the *Boston Commercial Bulletin* gives careful tables of wages of sixty-two grades of operatives, making "the average wages of woolen mill operatives in Massachusetts forty per cent. higher than in 1860."

COST OF LIVING AND WAGES.

Carrol D. Wright, *Chief of Massachusetts Bureau of Statistics*, gives a statement, in March, 1881, of comparative wages and costs of living of a weaver with a wife and three children in that State, and in Lancashire, England, on the same work in cotton mills, basing his statements on reports of Consuls and other good authority. The result gives the Massachusetts weaver above costs of food, rent and fuel, $2.30 per week, the Lancashire weaver 22½ cents. A cotton spinner's surplus would be $5.79 here, and $2.98 in the Blackburn mills, in England. The *London Times*, July, 1880, discussing the prospects of free trade in the United States, said :

"The United States do not approach the question from the same point of view as ourselves. The object of their statesmen is not to secure the largest amount of wealth for the country generally, *but to keep up, by whatever means, the standard of comfort among the laboring classes.*"

This is fair testimony, from a great English journal, of the benefit of our protective policy to our workmen ; but we also secure "the largest amount of wealth for the country" by that policy.

Exceptional circumstances vary costs as compared to wages. For instance, Mr. Wright's Report in 1882 gives increase of wages since 1878 seven per cent.; increase of cost of living in his State, 22 per cent. Very poor crops of grass, fruits and vegetables, with consequent high prices, explains this. Usual crops will make the

Wages and Protection. 143

prices of the farmer less and the costs of the operatives less also. For a long term of years the operatives' condition is better here than in any other country, as the following facts show:

SAVINGS BANK DEPOSITS AT HOME AND IN ENGLAND.

The *Detroit Post and Tribune* gives, from official reports, the aggregate deposits in the savings banks in Maine, New Hampshire, Vermont, Massachusetts, Rhode Island, Connecticut, New York, New Jersey and California for the years 1850, 1860, 1870 and 1881:

Deposits in 1850	$ 43,295,604
Deposits in 1860	148,546,876
Deposits in 1870	547,161,699
Deposits in 1881	787,432,993

Reducing all this to a gold standard to be fully accurate, and we have:

Year.	Amount of deposits, gold value.	Increase each 10 years in gold.
1850	$ 42,295,604	
1860	148,546,876	$106,251,272
1870	476,030,678	327,483,802
1881	787,432,993	311,402,311

From the foregoing it can be seen that the increase of deposits in these savings banks, at gold values, was more than three times greater under the first ten years of protection than it was in the so-called free trade 10 years.

In 34 years of free trade, so says the *News*, a Detroit free trade paper, the increase of deposits in all the savings banks of Great Britain has been $350,000,000. In 21 years of protection in the United States these deposits have increased $628,000,000 in nine States.

The Rhode Island savings banks in 1882 had 112,472 depositors, and those of Connecticut 225,366—or about one-third of the population. The total deposits in these two manufacturing States was $134,000,000. It is a significant fact that the amount of deposits and the number of depositors is largest in manufacturing sections, showing that the operatives are saving money.

Hon. W. A. Russell, M. C., of Massachusetts, in a Congressional speech in April, 1882, made the following comparison, which shows the ability of American operatives to live better, as they do, than the English, *and yet to put in bank seven times as much money to their numbers as is deposited by English workmen in Manchester.*

"Lowell has a population of 60,000, the largest in the State or in the United States wholly engaged in the manufacture of textile fabrics, and therefore well illustrates the condition of the industrial classes in our New England manufacturing centres.

"Of the 60,000 inhabitants 22,559 are employed in the various corporations and mills. There are six savings banks, with a total deposit of $11,646,212 to the credit of 33,408 depositors. Of this number 1,735 are depositors of amounts above $300, and 31,673 depositors of $300 and under, showing how general the habit of saving has become among our people, and what a large proportion of the funds in the savings banks are the earnings of the wage laborers. I have it from authority that fully seven-eights of the deposits in these savings banks are the laid-by earnings of the wage laborers.

"In Lawrence, with a population of 40,000, grown up wholly out of manufacturing and now supported by it, there are 13,000 operatives, three savings banks with $5,000,000 deposits, and 13,728 depositors.

"Manchester, England, corresponds with these two cities in its occupations, more nearly than any other: With a population of 341,508, it has in its various savings banks £1,434,140 or

$6,883,872; a city three and a half times as large as Lowell and Lawrence, and less than one-half the amount of deposits in its savings institutions."

WOMAN'S ELEVATION.

In this whole protective question the interest of woman is really as great as that of man, and in a day when so much thought is given to her elevation this should be borne in mind. Every woman should be a protectionist, for free trade degrades her even more than it does man. In this country her wages are quite as much above the British level as his. The lower wages of the English workman drive wife and children into the factory, and thus deprive the children of a home atmosphere and a mother's care. In Great Britain and Ireland, in 1870, there were six males to one female engaged in agricultural labor, in the United States, fourteen to one. In Great Britain and Ireland the proportion of men to women, in manufacturing, mechanical and mining industries, was two to one, in this country seven to one. The proportion of children under sixteen is four times greater there than here. The larger pay of our factory workmen enables the mother to be in her home, where her children need her in their tender years. For girls, or married women who choose factory work, the pay is better, and a more self-respecting and womanly life possible. Of course equal pay for equal work is justice, and usage does not give that to woman, nor does protection directly reach or change that usage, but it helps to better pay than free trade, and that is a lever to open the way to all else. In Massachusetts mills and shops women earned $30,000,000 in 1875, averaging over $300 each in the year.

The following is from the New York *Sun:*

EDITOR OF THE SUN—*Sir:* I found this advertisement in the Dublin *Freeman's Journal* of the 15th inst.:

WANTED—Strong, humble girl to assist in minding children and go of messages; age 15; 8s per quarter. Apply at 59 Harcourt St., 11 o'clock to 2, Monday.

For minding the children and running on errands the "strong, humble girl" will receive $8 a year, or 67 cents a month. Happy land!

B. F. F.

NEW YORK, February 20, 1882.

Consul-General Shaw, in his report from Manchester, referring to the successful efforts recently made by English ladies to encourage English manufactured goods to the exclusion of the foreign, which had for some time destroyed the fashionable use of alpaca goods of Bradford make, reads American ladies the following instructive protective lecture :

"It may be worthy of consideration how far American ladies can foster and develop American manufactures by similar patriotic and national action in our own country. The field for such wise and peaceful revolution is a wide and rich one, and considerate co-operation among our representative social leaders would have a powerful influence in creating a demand for special lines of American dress goods. It is high time American ladies should set *American fashions* and cease to follow the lead of *foreign fashion makers* beyond the sea!"

WAGES IN NEWARK AND PAISLEY—IN THE CLYDE SHIP-YARDS.

To the Editor of the New York Tribune:

SIR: Referring to the letter from Mr. Porter which appeared in last Sunday's *Tribune*, we would be obliged by your publishing the following table received from Clark & Co. by cable to-day, showing the actual average wages paid by them in Paisley, Scot-

Wages and Protection.

land, with which table we unite the wages we pay for the same work in Newark, New Jersey. These facts require no comment:

Weekly Wages in Newark.		Weekly Wages in Paisley.	
Cop-winders...	$8.00	Cop-winders...14s. or	$3.50
Finishers...	5.50	Finishers...10s. or	2.50
Reelers...	8.00	Reelers...17s. or	4.25
Spoolers...	8.00	Spoolers...13s. or	3.25
Foremen...	20.00	Foremen...28s. or	7.00
Pickers...	7.00	Pickers...16s. 6d. or	4.12
Hank-winders...	7.00	Hank-winders...15s. or	3.75

CLARK THREAD CO.,
By William Clark, Treasurer.
NEW YORK, January, 25, 1883.

Robert P. Porter writes the *New York Tribune* that he found that the pay-roll of one of the leading Clyde ship-yards contained the names of 1,600 men during the last two weeks of November, including foremen and apprentices, and that the amount it called for was £4,000, or £2,000 per week. This gave an average for each man of $6.25 a week. The average pay of skilled workmen was $7.50 a week, and that of unskilled laborers $2.50 a week. The census returns of the United States show that in 1880 there was paid out for wages in all kinds of ship-building in this country $12,800,000, which was divided among 21,330 hands, giving each about $600 per annum, or nearly twice as much as is paid on the Clyde.

Mr. Carroll D. Wright, Chief of the Bureau of Statistics of Labor of Massachusetts, states that the weekly earnings of a Massachusetts weaver are $6\frac{8}{10}$ per cent. greater than the weekly earnings of a weaver in England.

Hon. Jonathan Chace, from Rhode Island, a practical business man in cotton manufacture, estimates the pay of our cotton mill operatives about 62 per cent. above that of England, and sharply controverts the statement made by Mr. Wright as to the comparative weekly earnings here and there.

Mr. Wm. C. Wyckoff, secretary of the Silk Association of America, estimates that the average wages paid in the manufacture of silk goods in the United States are about 100 per cent. greater than in England.

J. W. HINTON.

In an address before the Wisconsin Legislature, at Madison, in 1881, John W. Hinton, of Milwaukee, alluding to the charge that factories were monopolies and oppressors of labor, cited the North Chicago Rolling Mill Company, "which will pay out in 1881 $3,000,000 in wages to workingmen. The president of that company, O. W. Potter, said, when addressing the iron and steel makers at Pittsburg, in May, 1879 : 'Pay your laborers well, and by your exhibition of faith in them you will always get faithful services from them.' Not very long since a prominent free trade member of Parliament, Mr. Huskisson, asserted publicly : 'To give capital a fair remuneration, the price of labor must be kept down.' The *London Times* declared that in England 'manhood became a drug and population a nuisance.' But Potter said to that meeting in Pittsburg : 'Every man of you have more or less men in your employ who know much more about many details of your business than you do, and who in a quiet way save their salaries every day; and these men you know and have confidence in, and would and do entrust them with your property.' By a tariff protecting American labor you make the artisan, as a citizen, a safer depository of the franchise than though abject dependence or gaunt poverty grimly shadowed his every footstep."

He also alluded to the monthly payment, at Bay View Iron Mills, Milwaukee, of $70,000 in wages, at rates over 50 per cent. above those paid in England.

COMPARATIVE TAXATION.

The excessive taxation of the working man by tariffs, &c., is often spoken of by free traders. Mr. Greg, an eminent Englishman, estimates that the English working classes are taxed by tariffs and excise taxes twenty-six shillings, or $6.50 yearly. Mr. Leffingwell, an American, writing in the *Contemporary Review*, London, makes the tax on an American of the same class in like manner $3 per year. Such estimates only approximate to accuracy, but show the assertions to be groundless. The legislation of this country is not perfect by any means, but it favors the people in its tariffs and taxes, more than that of England or of other lands.

STATEMENTS AT NATIONAL TARIFF CONVENTIONS AT CHICAGO AND NEW YORK.

In November, 1882, Tariff Conventions were held, first in Chicago and then in New York a fortnight later. Both were national in character, their members representing many industries and coming from the East and West and South. Some 200 delegates were at Chicago and over 600 at New York. An interesting part of their proceedings was the brief statements of the condition of each industry. In this connection such as related to labor are partly given.

The Chicago statements are first in order. Mr. E. S. Hartshorn, of Troy, New York, spoke of flax-spinning:

"I am engaged in flax-spinning, and with that business, as it exists at present here and in Europe, I am quite familiar. The labor for which we pay $100,000 annually can be had in Great Britain for $40,000. Are not the farmers surrounding our village, and the merchants, artisans, doctors, lawyers, boarding house keepers, house owners, &c., better off with $100,000 paid to the operatives in our works than if only $40,000 were paid ?"

Mr. Stowell, of Appleton, Wisconsin:

"Mr. President, I represent the paper interest, and our machinery chews up a great many jute butts and much tow flax every year. For our machine tenders, as they are technically called, the men that tend the machinery that runs off the paper, who receive in England five dollars and eighty cents a week, Germany, three dollars, we pay fifteen dollars a week. Rag engine men are paid in England five dollars and eighty cents, we pay thirteen dollars and a half a week. Bleachers are paid four dollars and thirty-five cents in England, and we pay nine dollars. Young boys and girls that attend to the paper as it comes off the machine, cutter-hands they are called, who cut and fold it, are paid in England two dollars and a half a week, and we pay four dollars and a half. The rag-pickers, girls who pick over and assort the rags, in England, two dollars a week, and we pay three dollars."

The President:

"The pottery interests are represented here. Mr. Laughlin, of East Liverpool, Ohio, and Mr. Knowles are present."

Mr. Knowles:

"We represent the manufacture of earthenware, and while a little selfish, are protectionists on a broad basis, and believe in protecting in proportion as the article produced represents labor.

"We have compiled some statistics of prices paid in our particular branch in Europe compared with what is paid here. The difference is greater on the articles that are most used, which would make it really in favor of the workman to a still greater extent; but the average on all the products will be about one hundred and fifty per cent; or, where they pay one dollar we pay two dollars and fifty cents for the same labor."

His table of wages, too long to insert, is carefully prepared and amply makes good his statement as to workmen's pay in a large industry—far more important than is supposed.

Wages and Protection.

Mr. Jerome spoke of jute butts imported, and the burning of flax straw in Iowa and elsewhere:

"I have a superintendent who has been in India very recently, and he gives me the facts. The very jute butts that are handled there at fourteen cents a day are brought over here as ballast, and pay a duty of a little more than a quarter of a cent a pound. That is the competition that the grangers have to contend with, and that is why he wants a duty on jute butts; and he will have to burn his flax until that duty comes. And instead of one hundred and forty thousand tons destroyed, there is more than five hundred thousand raised, and more than four hundred and fifty thousand tons burned and rotted and wasted when it should be used to-day."

Mr. Shuman, of Indiana, sent by three hundred workingmen, declared himself a protectionist and said he was highly pleased with the sayings and acts of the convention.

NEW YORK CONVENTION.

At the New York Tariff Convention like statements were made.

Alexander H. Jones, of Philadelphia, a well-known manufacturer of chemicals, reported as follows:

"Here are some figures as to daily wages paid in a Philadelphia factory and at St. Helen's, England, in a like establishment:

	America.	England.	Difference.
Acid makers............................	$ 1 50	$1 08	$ 42
Firemen	2 00	1 44	56
Ordinary laborers......................	1 33	84	49
Furnace men	2 00	1 44	56
Bricklayers............................	2 50@3 00	2 16	34@84
Carpenters.............................	2 25	1 40	85
Stone masons.........................	2 75	1 92	83
Fitters	2 75	1 44	1 31
Blacksmiths...........................	3 00	1 20	1 80

"Compare this difference with the total amount of wages paid by our chemical industry in the census year and it shows an excess of $7,554,900, paid in wages to 29,405 American hands, over English wages for the same work."

G. B. Stebbins, of Detroit, reported over 50,000 men employed in Michigan lumber camps, saw mills and salt works, at wages over twenty-five per cent. higher than are paid just across the lake and river in Canada. These wages aggregate $25,000,000 yearly or $5,000,000 more than Canadians pay for the same work.

In Michigan iron ore beds and copper mines and works on Lake Superior, 15,000 workmen get two dollars a day, double European pay. The yearly amount of their earnings is $9,000,000; excess over European earnings $4,500,000.

JOHN JARRETT—PETER COOPER.

At a large labor protection meeting in Cooper Institute, New York, Feb. 25th, 1883, under the auspices of associations of working men, John Jarrett, of Pittsburgh, President Amalgamated Association of Iron and Steel Workers, and others spoke. From Mr. Jarrett's address a paragraph must suffice :

"Now it happens I was born on the other side of the water, and I am pretty well conversant with the methods of living there, and I know pretty well what free trade has done for that country. The difference in ratio of prices at which they have to sell their products in England and the prices in this country is largely in our favor. The puddler receives as his standard wages all through the north of England 7 shillings 6 pence a ton, while here our men receive about $5.50. There he receives but one-twentieth of the price that commodity brings in the market ; and our men receive $5.50 for that same iron that brings on the market $56 ; in other words, we get $5.50 for our puddler, and the manufacturer gets $56, and the English puddler gets only $2 out of $35. You see, then, how largely it is in favor of our men, and the ratio carries itself all the way through."

The venerable philanthropist Peter Cooper sent a letter to the meeting, a valuable sentence of which is given:

"I have noticed in my own business life, extending over a period of nearly seventy years, that every reduction of the tariff (or 'the tariff for revenue only' plan) has brought wretchedness and ruin. It is the natural effect from such a cause. Nothing is more certain than that the advocacy of free trade comes from foreigners who want to break up our industries. They have done it several times already, and they want to do it again. The laborers of the Old World get barely enough to keep body and soul together, and that is the condition in which the advocates of free trade are trying to place our laborers, and it behooves every man to do all he can to deter Congress from the endeavor."

A resolution was adopted with hearty unanimity, calling on the people "to preserve a tariff that protects living wages."

This chapter may fitly close with the testimony of the New York correspondent of the London *Ironmonger*, who is instructed to investigate the iron trade in America and report to this English journal for their information. In the *Ironmonger* of October 9th, 1881, he makes this plain and forcible statement:

"*The plain truth of the matter is that about all that protection protects is labor.* With the same rates of wages there are but few things produced here at all which could not be produced in the United States as cheaply as in England. The chief advantage of protection is that it enables the workingman to live a great deal better than his English competitor, by making his labor more valuable. The manufacturers say they would suffer from the withdrawal of protection chiefly through the lowered ability of the masses of the people to consume; but that, so far as the cost of production is concerned, they could meet any competition with their improved machinery, and *with labor as cheap as it would be under free trade.*"

CHAPTER XI.

OPINIONS AND STATEMENTS OF EMINENT MEN.

The necessity of a protective system for the States was a main subject of deliberation at the first convention, in 1786, of delegates at Annapolis, met to consider the formation of a Constitution, and also at the convention of 1787, in which the Constitution was framed.

Washington, as President, met the first Congress clad in a suit of domestic manufacture, and the second Act passed by that Congress had the following preamble:

"WHEREAS, It is necessary for the support of Government, for the discharge of the debts of the United States, and for the encouragement and protection of manufactures, that duties be laid on goods, wares and merchandise imported. Be it enacted," etc., etc.

This bill was signed by Washington, July 4, 1789. Jefferson, made President by a rival party, was too broad in his views to differ from Washington on this great question. In his second message, he said:

"To cultivate peace, and maintain commerce and navigation in all their lawful enterprises, to foster our fisheries, as nurseries of navigation and for the nurture of man, and to protect the manufactures adapted to our circumstances—these are the landmarks by which we are to guide ourselves."

President Madison's special message, May 23, 1809:

"The revision of our commercial laws, proper to adapt them to the arrangement which has taken place with Great Britain, will doubtless engage the early attention of Congress. It will be worthy at the same time of their just and provident care *to make such alteration in the laws as will especially protect and foster the several branches of manufacture.*"

Benjamin Franklin:

"Every manufacturer encouraged in our country makes part of a market for provisions within ourselves and saves so much money to this country as must otherwise be exported for the manufactures he supplies."

Andrew Jackson, December 7th, 1830, Second Annual Message as President of the United States:

"The power to impose duties on imports originally belonged to the several States. The right to adjust these duties with a view to the encouragement of domestic branches of industry is so completely identical with that power that it is difficult to suppose the existence of the one without the other. The States have delegated their whole authority over imports to the Federal Government without limitation or restriction, saving the very inconsiderable restriction relating to their inspection laws. This authority having thus entirely passed from the States, the right to exercise it for the purpose of protection does not exist in them; and consequently if it be not possessed by the General Government it must be extinct. Our political system would thus present the anomaly of a people stripped of the right to foster their own industry and to counteract the most selfish and destructive policy which might be adopted by foreign nations. This surely cannot be the case; this indispensable power thus surrendered by the States must be within the scope of the authority on the subject expressly delegated to Congress.

"In this conclusion I am confirmed as well by the opinions of Presidents Washington, Jefferson, Madison, and Monroe, who have each repeatedly recommended the exercise of this right under the Constitution, as by the uniform practice of Congress, the continued acquiescence of the States, and the general understanding of the people."

President J. Q. Adams' Fourth Annual Message, December 2, 1828:

"The great interests of an agricultural, commercial, and manufacturing nation, are so linked in union together that no permanent cause of prosperity to one of them can operate without extending its influence to the others. All these interests are alike under the protecting power of legislative authority, and the duties of the representative bodies are to conciliate them in harmony together."

Henry Clay, speech in the House of Representatives, March 30 and 31, 1824:

"The proposition to be maintained by our adversaries is, that manufactures, without protection, will, in due time, spring up in the country and sustain themselves, in competition with foreign fabrics, however advanced the arts and whatever the degree of protection may be in foreign countries. Now, I contend that this proposition is refuted by all experience, ancient and modern, in every country. If I am asked why unprotected industry should not succeed in a struggle with protected industry, I answer, the fact has ever been so, and that is sufficient; I reply that uniform experience evinces that it cannot succeed in such a struggle, and that is sufficient. If we speculate on the causes of this universal truth, we may differ about them. Still the indisputable fact remains."

Henry Clay, speech in United States Senate, Feb. 2, 3 and 6, 1832:

"In short, sir, if I were to select any term of seven years since the adoption of the present Constitution which exhibited a scene of the most wide spread dismay and desolation, it would be exactly that term of seven years which immediately preceded the establishment of the tariff of 1824."—"If the term of seven years were to be selected of the greatest prosperity which this people have enjoyed since the establishment of their present Constitution, it would be exactly that period of seven years which immediately followed the passage of the tariff of 1824."—"And is the fact not indisputable, that all essential objects of consumption affected by the tariff are cheaper and better since the act of 1824, than they were for several years prior to that law? Let us look into some particulars. The total consumption of bar iron in the United States is supposed to be about 146,000 tons, of which 112,866 tons are made within the country, and the residue imported. The measure of protection extended to this necessary article was never adequate until the passage of the act of 1828; and what has been the consequence? The annual increase of quantity, since that period, has been in the ratio of near 25 per cent., and the whole sale price of bar iron in the Northern cities was, in 1828, $105 per ton; in 1829, $100; in 1830, $90; and in 1831, from $85 to $75— constantly diminishing."

Daniel Webster, speech at mass meeting at Albany, August 27, 1844:

"The term (protection) was well understood in our colonial history, and if we go back to the history of the Constitution, and of the convention which adopted it, we shall find that everywhere, when masses of men were assembled, and the wants of the people were brought forth into prominence, the idea was held up that domestic industry could not prosper, manufactures and the mechanic arts could not advance, the condition of the common country could not be carried up to any considerable elevation, unless there should be one government, to lay one rate of duty upon imports throughout the Union, from New Hampshire to Georgia; regard to be had, in laying this duty, to the protection of American labor and industry. I defy the man in any degree conversant with history, in any degree acquainted with the annals of this country from 1787 to the adoption of the Constitution in 1789, to say that this was not a leading, I may almost say the leading, motive, South as well as North, for the formation of the new government. Without that provision in the Constitution it never could have been adopted."

John M. Berrien, United States Senator from Georgia, in 1843:

"1. The credit of the government was prostrate, and has been redeemed. Its stock is again above par. 2. The treasury was empty; it is now replenished. 3. The commerce and navigation of the country have increased. 4. Its agricultural condition has improved. 5. There has been a marked improvement of our great staple (cotton). 6. A reduction in the prices of almost all, if not absolutely of every article of consumption. 7. To crown the whole, every branch of industry has been stimulated to increased activity, and confidence has been restored. These things, I apprehend, are true. The tariff of 1842 has been in efficient operation but little more than a year, and these effects have followed."

Horace Greeley, Essays on Political Economy, 1869, disposes of the "monopoly" absurdity in a terse and plain way, as follows:

"But with what reason, with what justice, does one say that an impost or tax on imported iron or nails, cloth or cutlery, creates a monopoly? A great many of our countrymen were previously employed in making these articles. In what sense is a monopoly accorded to any or the whole of them together? Do we not know that, not only will each of them sell as his own interest prompts, and increase his product so fast and so far as he can do so with profit, but that any one else who will may embark in the business whenever he shall see fit? How can A have had conferred on him by law a monopoly of that which B, C, D, and all the rest of the alphabet, are not only at perfect liberty to embark in whenever they will, but which this very act strongly tends to invite them to engage in, having been passed for that express purpose?"

Henry C. Carey, Principles of Social Science:

"The laborer *must* sell his potential energies, be they what they may, or perish for want of food. In regard to no commodity, therefore, is the effect resulting from the presence or absence of competition so great as in relation to human force. Two men competing for its purchase, its owner becomes a free man. The two competing for its sale become enslaved. The whole question of freedom or slavery for man is, therefore, embraced in that of competition."—"A bushel of corn is *worth* as much in Illinois or Iowa as in the neighborhood of Paris or of London; and the sole reason why it *sells* for only a fourth or a fifth as much is, that the farmer is burdened with the cost of sending it to market. Bring the market to him by opening the great coal and ore deposits of Indiana and Illinois, Missouri and Michigan, and then not only will he be relieved of the necessity for looking to distant markets, but it will become impossible for him to supply them, because the price at home will be on a level with that abroad. The change thus effected would count to the farmers of the country to the extent of many hundreds of millions of dollars, and at no distant day it would be reckoned by thousands of millions."

M. Thiers, speech in the Corps Legislatif, Paris, January 26, 1870.

"France has her consumers within herself. Her market does not depend upon a cannon-shot fired in Europe. And for exportation she has her beautiful products. England on the contrary, has an artificial existence. She depends upon the doings of the United States; upon the doings of her colonies, which already oppose her with hostile tariffs. May not the day come when her immense production will find no purchasers? She produces ten times as much as her consumption! This little island, in the words of Fox, embraces the world. True; but when she embraces the world she is vulnerable everywhere.

"Such was the situation of Holland in the seventeenth century, which had realized a prodigy almost as marvelous. What was needed to make Holland, which gave laws to France, descend from this lofty place? It needed only fifty years. It needed only a Navigation Act in England; it needed only a Colbert in France.

"God forbid that I should predict for England such a destiny; but, I repeat it, her existence, which depends upon consumers, which she seeks everywhere without herself, is less solid than that of France, which has her consumers in her own bosom."

E. B. Ward, Detroit, Michigan:

"When a nation fosters and protects its own resources and interests through its national laws, it prospers. If the laws are so framed as to give other nations the advantage, either through their superior skill, cheap labor, or cheap and abundant capital, it suffers. When a nation separates by great distances the producers of raw materials from the consumers, the producers practically pay the transportation, and become poor, while a few forwarders, traders, and carriers become rich at the expense of the producer and consumer. When a nation diversifies its means for the employment and utilization of all its laborers, prosperity and wealth ensue, while the nation and people who confine themselves principally to one employment become poor and dependent."

David H. Mason, Chicago, Ill.:

"Foreign producers are not subject to our laws, nor amenable to the processes of our courts, nor obligated to serve on our juries, nor liable to be drafted into our armies, nor bound to contribute to our internal taxes, nor answerable for non-performance of any of the duties of American citizenship. They are total aliens to our national commonwealth. To permit them to sell their merchandise in our home markets free of all tariff charge, free of all local burdens, and free of all allegiance to our government, would be to exalt perfect strangers above the heads of its own patriotic people in privilege. The foreigner, abiding in a distant land, and often hostile at heart to our republican institutions, has no right to ask to be placed on a dead level of commercial benefits with our citizens, who bear a round of local burdens incident to those institutions—burdens from which he is exempt. It has cost a vast amount of sacrifice, an immense aggregate of exertion, and an incalculable investment of capital, on the part of our population, through a number of generations, to transform a perfect wilderness into the most opulent and the most desirable of the world's markets. Why should the total alien, without any participation in developing our resources, without sharing in the support of our government, without a personal stake in the welfare of our Union, be allowed to be an exceptionally favored beneficiary of all that toil and effort? There is no way in which he can be compelled to compensate our nationality for the high privilege of admission to our domestic markets except through duties on imports. Only by the imposition of such charges, made adequate to the purpose, can the unequal conditions of competition be equalized between the alien and the citizen, meeting as rivals in trade upon our soil."

Joseph Wharton, Philadelphia, Pa.:

"The old-fashioned way of gaining population from a neighboring country by invading it and carrying off its inhabitants as slaves is no longer practiced by civilized nations, and the acquisition of territory by similar means is perhaps not so frequent as it once was, but the newer style of aggrandizement by winning the wealth of a neighbor through industrial assaults and trade invasions is now in the fullest activity.

"In this modern and highly civilized style of warfare, improved machinery takes the place of improved artillery; the enemy's forces—his industrial population—are driven from their guns by missiles of textiles and metal wares, and are destroyed in their homes by starvation rather than by bullets in the field.

'It is clear that the patriotism which can sleep through this industrial warfare and suffer this trade spoilation, and can only be roused into activity by the danger and passion of flagrant war; which can vote the public money to maintain rarely used armies, navies, and forts, but cannot give the slightest aid or comfort to the real and constant defenders of its country's independence—its industrial soldiers—is a patriotism belonging to periods long gone by, and is of little more present use than a bow and arrow. The spirit of loyalty is forever the same, but it must now learn to promote its conntry's welfare by the arts of peace, pursuing its ancient and honorable aim by the new methods."

Professor Francis Bowen, Harvard College, Cambridge, Mass. (Political Economy, pp. 491-92):

"But on this great question between free trade and protection the arguments relating to pecuniary loss and gain (important as they are) do not merit so much notice as those respecting the devotion of the greater part of the people to skilled or rude labor. * * * Viewed in this light, the question seems to be one between progress in civilization and the arts, or a gradual return, I will not say to barbarism, but to that imperfect stage of civilization which exists in all countries where the people are almost exclusively devoted to agriculture. The best legislative policy is that which will most effectually develop all the natural advantages of a country, whether mental or material. It is as wasteful, to say the least, to allow mechanical skill and inventive genius to remain unemployed, as to permit water-power to run without turning mill wheels, or minerals to remain in the ore, or forests to stand where cotton and grain might grow luxuriantly. * * * To give full scope to all varieties of taste, genius, and temperament; to foster inventive talent; to afford adequate encouragement to all the arts, whether mechanical or those usually distinguished as the fine arts; to concentrate the people * * * within the sphere of the humanizing influences and larger means of mental culture and social improvement * * * in cities and large towns;—these are objects which deserve at least as much attention as the inquiry where we can buy calicoes cheapest, or how great pecuniary sacrifice must be made before we can make our own railroad iron.

"I see not how these ends can be obtained in a country like ours * * * without throwing over our manufacturing industry, at least for half a century to come, the broad shield of an effective protecting tariff. * * * * * * *

"A protective duty prevents agriculture from being so overdone as to render raw material the only article of export, and to depress its price so low that, though the people have a rude abundance of food and other mere necessaries, they are deprived of most of the comforts and elegancies of life ; * * * the cost of commodities will be less than if the duty had not been imposed; its general effect is to stimulate invention, to multiply the productive arts, and to enlarge the sources of national opulence."

John L. Hayes, Cambridge, Mass. :

"The assertion of England that protective doctrines are opposed to the philosophical and practical judgment of the present period, is not to be believed, because England is deeply interested in making the world accept this fallacy. With her teeming and starving, and now restless and discontented population, her very existence depends upon keeping open the foreign outlets for her manufactures, and receiving, at cheap rates, the raw material of other nations. By creating a current of sentiment which will tend to a removal by other nations of restrictions upon the entry of her goods, she secures a triple purpose, the occupation of foreign markets, the means of increasing the prices of her goods by crushing out competing manufactures, and the cheapening of the desired products of agriculture, which is sure to result from the abandonment of domestic manufactures in all the countries into which her goods can enter without restriction. England stands forth not so much as the great exemplar, but as the great *propagandist* of free trade. To engraft this policy upon other nations, is the paramount idea of British statesmanship. It governs all her diplomacy, is never lost sight of in her legislation, and is avowed by all her ministers. All English literature is tinged by the political philosophy inspired by this idea. Her press reiterates day by day its platitudes concerning the progress of liberal ideas, and its paradoxes concerning the unselfishness of British commerce, not to affect opinion in England, which is always fixed in the direction of interest, but to create opinion outside of England. During the last century an institution was founded in England, under the style of "The Society for Propagating the Gospel in Foreign Parts," whose practical benevolence is attested by many churches still standing in this country, erected by its funds. The great missionary enterprise to which England of to-day is devoted is the propagation in "foreign parts" (especially in the United States) of the doctrine of a political religion,—the gospel of free trade. Its tracts are the essays of British economists; its colporteurs, her commercial traders; its foreign missionaries, the representatives of the press of our leading commercial city; and its churches, our bonded warehouses. No influence which can contribute to the spread of this religion is despised; no accessible organ which can affect opinion abroad remains unsubsidized."

Stephen Colwell, report as United States Revenue Commissioner, to the Secretary of the Treasury, 1866:

"The purchasing power of a people who have duly mingled manufactures with agriculture is tenfold that of a purely agricultural community. They purchase of each other. The population of Great Britain and the United States is not far from thirty millions each, yet the internal trade of the United States is tenfold greater in value than all our foreign trade, Great Britain included. The strength and wealth of a country should be measured by the quantity and value of its own productions which it consumes, and not by what it sends abroad. Massachusetts and Philadelphia contribute to the consumption of the United States more than all Europe; so also the City of New York and New Jersey. The trade between Pennsylvania, New Jersey and New York on the one side, and New England on the other, vastly exceeds our trade with Europe. Like facts may be found in the statistics of every State and county."

Robert E. Thompson, Professor of Social Science and National Economy in the University of Pennsylvania. (Social Science, etc.—page 271):

"Is it 'natural' that any nation should keep its farms on one continent and its workshops on another? Is it 'natural' that cotton, on its way from the grower to the weaver, should go half way round the globe and back again? Is it 'natural' that a large part of the race should be employed in carrying bulky articles—raw materials and coarse goods—from some countries to others in the same climate and of the same general capacity? Is it 'natural' that a country with millions of tons of iron on the surface of her soil, and square miles of coal not far below it, should send thousands of miles for railroad iron? * * * Protection is natural resistance to an unnatural state of things."

Hon. W. D. Kelley, M. C., in Congress, May, 1882:

"The framers of our tariff regarded all forms of American labor, and, placing a duty upon the primary element of an article if of native production, advanced the rate as the article was advanced by an increased expenditure of labor.

"In this they followed not only the teachings of social science, but the example of France, who still maintains many of the provisions of her tariff law of 1793. Her tariff from the days of Colbert has been a series of graded duties, increasing with the increased labor involved in each step of the advancement of the article. Let me invite the attention of the committee to the result of the industrial stability secured by this permanence of wisely adjusted rates of duty. Dynasties have risen and perished; the doctrine of the divine right of kings was swept away by the breath of a new-born democracy; an empire subdued the violence of this new-born giant, and restored monarchy succeeded the empire. But, though political revolutions have occurred at brief intervals throughout the century, the industries of France have been stable, the French people have prospered and French industry and art have conquered the world by their excellence and elegance; and it is still true that a pound of cotton manufactured in France, and beautified by her cultivated artisans, will pay for scores of pounds of coarse and adulterated British fabrics."

Abraham Lincoln, Illinois, 1832:

"I am in favor of the internal improvement system, and a high protective tariff."

He held the same views all his life.

CHAPTER XII.
COMMON INTEREST INSTEAD OF SECTIONAL JEALOUSY.

The more we study the interdependence, intimate relations, and common interests of different parts of our wide country, the more we see the benefits of free and ready intercourse and exchange of products within our borders, and of a national protective policy beneficial alike to all.

In an able speech in Chicago, Hon. V. B. Denslow said : "The United States was the first to establish perfect free trade among all the people within one national boundary." France, as he says, not abolishing her interior custom houses, until 1793, and Germany not until from 1810 to 1830, under the advice of Frederick List, long a resident of that country, an able protectionist and a disciple and friend of Matthew Carey, of Philadelphia. England had duties discriminating against Ireland up to 1846.

It is a new evidence of the ability of the Fathers of our country in 1787 that they inaugurated protection in foreign commerce and free trade at home at the same time.

Free trade appeals to sectional jealousy; protection builds up national unity. Fifty years ago Southern free traders advocated that policy "to insure the British market for their cotton, prevent Northern manufactures, force a large number of Northern men into agriculture, multiply the growth and increase the price of provisions, to feed and clothe their slaves at cheaper rates." (See "Cotton is King, published and sold by subscription only, Augusta, Ga., 1830.") To-day Western free traders move as British wire-pullers wish, and try to set the West against the East, the plundered farmer against the robber manufacturer, class against class. The enlightened protectionist commends the East for its wise enterprise, and says to the West and South, "Go and do likewise."

NEW ENGLAND INDUSTRIES.

A native of New England, I made my home in the West years ago, and am satisfied, yet not unmindful of the advantages of my native land. Thus, I may be impartial.

Suppose we travel together over ground familiar to me, and keep our eyes open and thoughts awake, as all sensible people should when journeying.

Start eastward from New York over the New Haven Railroad. The land is thin but carefully cultivated, fine towns and villages are near each other, thrift and growth are manifest. The life overflowing from the great city may help this, but it lasts beyond the reach of that tide.

In these towns are mills and factories. In Bridgeport, for instance, are the great buildings where the Wheeler & Wilson sewing machines are made, and shops of other kinds. Reaching New Haven, the trade of sea and land, the gathered wealth of two hundred years, the colleges with their army of students may be counted, but we must add the factories and shops to know what keeps up the life and growth. Turn north to Hartford. It is the same along the road, and on reaching that beautiful city, we see again great manufactures and wondrous mechanism. Still, up the lovely valley of the Connecticut, and we find richer land, but narrow in extent, with rude hills on either side, and the blue mountains standing grandly against the sky, west and north. Reaching Springfield, its mills and shops for cotton, wool, paper, hardware, tools, and guns, give scope for inventive genius, varied employ to labor, activity to trade, and ready market at good prices for the products of the farms.

Look into the newspapers, and you see advertisements of dealers in Western produce, with their agents in Toledo, Chicago, and other cities, showing how these thousands of workmen reach out eager hands for the food wherewith we can fill them. Still north, at Holyoke, the river is spanned by a dam eleven hundred feet long; a canal sixty feet wide and twelve feet deep is opened, and along its banks are mills for wire, thread, paper, and cotton, with the stream tumbling over the rocks on the east, and the homes of thirty thousand people on the west.

At Northampton we find the old town, always beautiful, adding freshness and life to its beauty. Street-cars carry us to Florence, a suburb three miles westward, where delicate mechanism twists gossamer threads and finishes thousands of pounds of the famed "Nonotuck" sewing silk a month, paying 400 skilled men and women good wages. In a great shop, with a lookout from its upper windows over river and meadow and mountain, worth going far to see, are made hardware goods in large quantities. Pleasant homes, fine churches, a noble school house, a library open free to all, make up the village of three thousand people—intelligent, self-respecting, working men and women.

We have traveled a hundred and fifty miles, and might go farther with similar results and observations. On our way we have passed branch railroads, reaching into regions remote from cities, yet paying their way by carrying to factories among the hills the food that we produce, and bringing back the products of those factories, to find their way often to us.

Should we continue our journey, we should find that Worcester, "the heart of the commonwealth," with its excellent population, and a large share of intelligent mechanics among them, has large and varied manufactures. The Providence Railroad skirts the bank of the Blackstone river, passing through thirty miles of well-nigh continuous villages, so near neighbors are the mills along the rocky stream, and ends at the great centre of the industry and trade that have made little Rhode Island rich, with a soil so poor its people would starve unless fed from the Western prairies. Its mills, too, would close up unless the South sent them cotton.

Not only great corporations carry on business, but, in many a smaller shop among New England hills, a man of moderate means, or a few such combined, earn an independence, while men of superior skill and good habits not only add to the wealth of large employers, but gain a competence themselves.

By returns of births and deaths in Massachusetts, mortality is decreasing, and the average of health and length of life slowly reaching upward. Doubtless, there is weariness and pain among factory workers, as well as dullness and vice among the lower grades, but this is, unfortunately, the case elsewhere, and the results, on a broad scale, tell well for the influence of varied industry on the health and character of the people. Every new factory in the East benefits every farmer in the West and South, and our way is open to increase that benefit by increasing like industries in our midst.

The East, with experience, skill, and capital, are making fine fabrics, delicate tools, and admirable mechanism. We begin with simpler products, and our abundant food and fuel and raw materials will draw manufacturers to us with a force sure as gravitation, if we are timely and persistent in our efforts to that end.

THE SOUTH—A NEW ERA.

The South is entering upon a new era.

Its singular advantage is in the variety of its resources —lands on the coasts and river-bottoms of wonderful fertility, fitted for cotton, rice and sugar, and plains, and mountain valleys, and hills, yielding wheat and corn and grass of finest quality wait to be tilled; fruits, from the orange to the peach and apple, can be produced; swift streams are ready to serve man by turning many water-wheels; large rivers can be navigated far up to the interior; great mines of iron and copper, beds of coal and quarries of stone wait to be opened; vast forests stand ready to serve human needs; spacious bays and noble harbors are along thousands of miles of coast, on ocean and gulf, and the mild, yet salubrious air of its upper valleys favors vigor of body and mind. Such variety of resources and advantages can hardly be found, in a similar extent, on the globe.

The lesson is plain: diversify the industry of the people, that this varied wealth may be developed. This is the great work of to-day,—this is the industrial "reconstruction" of the South, by which will come employment, harmony, comfort, wealth, and the light and power of a growing civilization.

Under the old system, land was held in large tracts, and tilled for a few great staples, with little variety in its products; and those staples were exported to Europe and to the North. Even the raising of grain was neglected, and food imported for the laborers. Manufactures were little thought of, and all efforts given to the raising and export of these staples, robbing the soil of its wealth, with no return for the wholesale spoilation. No wonder the old planting States grew poor and men migrated from worn-out lands to newer regions, to begin again, on virgin soil, the exhaustive process and thus gain a living for themselves, but hand down a heritage of exhaustion to their children.

This system is of the past. Lands will be tilled for more varied crops, and a gradual change will substitute farms of moderate size, managed by their working owners and occupants for the great plantations. Grain will be raised for export as well as home use, and the risk of failure of crops lessened by their variety. Cotton factories, iron mills, and machine shops must be built, mines and coal-beds opened, and forests utilized, giving employ to all, attracting skill and capital, giving home markets for the farmer's produce, saving vast costs of transportation abroad, and paying back to the soil, in fertilizers, the wealth of which it has been robbed.

Such will be the new era, full of benefit and blessing. Men of the South, are you ready for your noble work? Women of the South, will you give the influence of your womanhood, helping upward to a better future?

A few facts touching the home consumption of cotton, will show the effect of legislation. In 1824 factories north of the Potomac used 110,000 bales, but in 1835 this had grown to 216,000, nearly doubling in seven years from 1828 and increasing four times as fast as the population. This growth was under a protective tariff. In 1842 the consumption was 267,000 bales, an increase of but 23 per cent., while population had increased 25 per cent. This slow increase was under a compromise tariff.

Of the crop of 1847-8, the home demand used 531,000 bales, nearly doubling in five years, and increasing six times as fast as population; this large increase being under a protective tariff again.

For three years, from 1857 to 1860, the average consumption was 668,000 bales, an increase of but 25 per cent. in ten years, while population had grown forty per cent.; this slow increase being again under the low tariff system of 1848. The South had started home manufactures a little, and in 1848 their cotton consumption had reached 100,000 bales, under a protective tariff, and the *Charleston Mercury* expressed the belief that in ten years the South would not export raw cotton; but that tariff was reduced, and the consumption went back to 87,500 bales in 1860. In 1860, by the census, there were 5,235,727 cotton-spindles in the country, and the increase up to 1864-5 was slight, if any, but in 1868 there were 7,000,000 spindles, and the home consumption had reached 900,000 bales, in the year ending September, 1868. This again was under a protective tariff. These facts tell their own story.

In 1868 the hardy lumbermen of Michigan fitted for market 750,000,000 feet of lumber, and the products of the mines and forests of that State were some $40,000,000. In 1880 they reached $75,000,000. The total product of all Massachusetts manufactures in 1880 was $631,000,000. In ten years, from 1855 to 1865, the farm products had grown from $50,000,000 to

$100,000,000, showing the benefit to the farm of the factory being a neighbor. This was in an old State, and on thin soil; with more room and richer resources the South can surely equal these results.

By returns of the National Association of Cotton Manufacturers and Planters, there were eighty-six cotton mills in the Southern States in 1868, running 215,000 spindles and using 41,500,000 pounds of cotton.

The increase of spindles from 1868 to 1880 was nearly three fold, or up to 600,000, and the Boston *Commercial Bulletin* said in 1874: "There is nothing visionary in the handsome dividends that the mills of Georgia are paying, even in these hard times."

Hon. Alexander H. Stephens wrote the *Philadelphia Press:*

"Suppose the cotton crop of my State (Georgia) should reach 500,000 bales, allowing 500 pounds to the bale, it would aggregate 250,000,000 pounds, which, at ten cents per pound, would make its value $25,000,000. This cotton manufactured into thread (which can be done more cheaply in Georgia than in Massachusetts and Rhode Island) and exported in this shape to the North and to Europe to be put into cloth, would amount in value to $75,000,000, instead of $25,000,000 when only the raw material is exported. Our future, therefore, is great and hopeful in prospect if our people are but true to themselves in working out their own high destiny."

The great Industrial Exhibition in Atlanta in 1880, gave cheering proofs of the growth of Southern skill and varied industry. In 1874 Louisville, Ky., had 500 manufacturing establishments, with $20,000,000 invested, $56,000,000 produced, and ten thousand workers employed. Tennessee iron is sold in all Western markets; Alabama iron is made into car wheels in Philadelphia, and its ore goes to Indiana furnaces. The Vulcan and

Tredegar works of Richmond, Va., ship their products to Cuba and South America, and make fish-bar bolts for Northern railways.

The iron product of Alabama increased 792 per cent., and that of Georgia 245 per cent., from 1870 to 1880. Thus "the good work goes bravely on," under the benign influence of a national protective policy. *With that policy, and with persistent effort on their part, the new era of diversified industry in the South is sure to come, full of blessing and benefit; but with free trade, or its near kin " tariff for revenue only," their efforts will be vain, and new troubles await them and all of us.*

Ex-Governor Bullock, of Atlanta, Georgia, now engaged in cotton manufacture, attended the Tariff Conventions in Chicago and New York last November. At Chicago he said :

"Visionary theories are disappearing before the substantial advance of accomplished facts. Here the East, the West and the South meet together with a common purpose and a common interest to foster and encourage such legislation as will by its protective features build up the mechanical industries whereby we can fabricate within the borders of our own country the natural products of our soil, our mines and of our forests, thereby securing an enhanced and diversified prosperity, by making sections and communities more homogeneous and less dependent upon artificial means of transportation.

"It is a trite saying, but none the less true, that the farmer needs the mechanic to consume his surplus of provisions, and the mechanic needs the farmer to use his surplus of fabrics.

"I have said this gathering marks an era. It is within the memory of the youngest man here that corn has been burned as fuel in this section, when underlying the fields upon which that corn was grown were veins of the finest coal.

"I regret to say that in my section we are to-day wearing out the points of plows not made at home, by dragging them through the iron ore that lays upon our hill-sides."

In a late speech in the Capitol at Washington, Hon. G. W. Hewitt, M. C., of Alabama, said :

"No great measure has promoted the general prosperity of the country to a greater extent than the protection of American labor and American industries. * * * New England farmers have prospered because they have factories near, and a market at their door for all they have to sell. The Alabama farmers are as much interested in the development of coal and iron, and the building of cotton mills, as any class of persons."

Mr. Hewitt spoke of the coal and iron of his State, "equal to a supply of the world for many centuries."

A WESTERN VIEW.

The *Indianapolis Journal* says :

"Nothing in the moral world is more certain than that the prosperity and welfare of the country demand a policy of judicious protection. It is the habit of some to dismiss the consideration of this subject with the remark that it concerns only the manufacturing interest, and consequently is interesting only to a class. There could be no greater mistake than this. It concerns all interests, the development of the whole country, and the prosperity of every individual. If protection is the true policy, as reason, experience, and facts prove it to be, the farmers of Indiana and the West are as much interested in its establishment as are the manufacturers of New England and the East. For it stands to reason that the development of manufactures means the creation of a home market for the products of the soil, with diversified industry and general prosperity.

"Suppose the case of a farmer without any market at all for his surplus products. Suppose him to be located in the midst of an extensive plain or valley, fertile and productive, but inaccessible and so completely cut off from the rest of the world that he would have no market at all. Not only would the results of his toil be greatly lessened by the impossibility of procuring labor-saving machinery and implements, but all that he produced over and above the wants of himself and family would be sheer waste,—dead loss for the lack of a market. The condition of such a farmer would be most deplorable. Second, suppose that instead of no market at all he had a very distant one, say a manufacturing city or town a hundred miles distant, and accessible only by country road. This would be an improvement, but still very far from a happy condition. The remoteness of the market and the difficulty of reaching it would prevent him from availing himself of it with any regularity. If other farmers were situated near it, he would be completely at their mercy. He could sell but very few articles, and would have to take the buyer's price. But, third, suppose a manufacturing town to spring up within a few miles of the farmer's house, and the means of communication such as to enable him to market his products every day or whenever it suited him. Now, he not only has a steady and reliable sale for all he can produce, at good prices, but he is encouraged to engage in branches of agriculture untried before, and to produce articles which he had never dreamed there was any demand for or any profit in. By the cheapening of many things which he needed, and which are now produced almost at his door, his labor is rendered more easy and productive, while the surplus produce which before was accustomed to decay on his hands now finds steady and profitable sale. To state the case in a nutshell, protection creates a home market for home products."

The aggregate value of the manufactures, leading mechanic arts and flouring mills included, of seven leading cities in the Northwest in 1880 was $587,000,000. (This includes Chicago, Milwaukee, St. Louis, Louisville, Detroit, Cincinnati and Cleveland; see U. S. census.) The great coal fields of Iowa must be utilized there. California and Oregon are beginning to manufacture woolens and iron, and with the growth of manufactures protective opinion gains. New York City is becoming a great centre of home industry as well as of foreign trade. The quarter of a million workmen this employs cannot be the dumb slaves of a policy that ends in low wages. The men who have invested over $150,000,000 in these establishments cannot sit quiet and see efforts for legislation which would discriminate against them and in favor of foreigners. So we find in New York, a great tariff convention and a strong industrial league.

The Chicago *Inter Ocean*, in commenting on the statistics of the census of 1880 relative to the manufactures of leading cities, says:

"It is important as showing the vast extent to which New York City is indebted for its commercial prestige to the fact that it is the centre of American manufactures. The total manufactures of the port of New York proper, including merely those of New York City, Jersey City, and Brooklyn, and excluding those of Paterson, Newark, Elizabeth, Yonkers, and other manufacturing suburbs of New York, are as follows:

Cities.	Establishments.	Capital.	Workers.	Annual product.
New York..........	11,162	$164,917,856	217,977	$488,209,248
Brooklyn...........	5,089	56,621,399	45,226	169,757,590
Jersey City........	555	11,329,915	10,688	59,581,541
Total.............	16,806	$232,869,170	273,891	$717,548,379

"The total imports and exports of merchandise at the port of York for 1880 were as follows:

Imports of merchandise.................$459,937,153
Exports of merchandise................. 385,506,602

Total............................$845,443,755

"It appears, therefore, that the annual product of the manufactures of New York City alone exceeds by $30,000,000 its entire imports, though these imports are for distribution over the entire country, and the aggregate annual product of the port of New York very nearly equals its entire imports and exports combined. Indeed, if the two manufacturing suburbs—Newark and Paterson—are included, the total annual product considerably exceeds the entire imports and exports of that great mart which has been supposed by some to live out of its foreign trade. The fact is that New York, like the rest of the country, is acquiring a volume of business in connection with its manufactures and domestic trade which, in relative importance, rises far above its foreign trade. The entire foreign trade of New York, import and export, probably does not support more than 100,000 out of its 1,250,000 people."

Philadelphia, with her longer established and more varied industries, aggregating $430,000,000, prizes the thrift and wealth they bring her people. It must be borne in mind that manufactures give employ to many more persons than mercantile business of a like amount does, or can.

A careful article in a late *International Review* shows that in 1850, in nine Western States—Ohio, Indiana, Illinois, Michigan, Wisconsin, Iowa, Missouri, Kansas, and Nebraska—there were 24,921 manufacturing establishments employing 110,501 persons, and producing $146,348,554 worth. In 1880 these had grown to 124,763, employing 755,286 persons, and producing $1,819,588,355 worth. In 1850 the Western States and territories had about 12 per cent. of the total investment of the United States in manufactures; in 1880, over 30 per cent., with 3,500,000 of their 20,000,000 people sustained by manufactures and mechanism, and purchasers of farm products.

An early settler, now owner in a large iron mill in a Western city, tells of an old and valued friend, a pioneer farmer, who was an earnest and honest free trader, opposed to "monopolists." He came one day for a visit, and they went through the mill together, talked of its product wages market for produce and the like, but no word of protection or free trade. Going back to the office the visitor sat silent and in absent thought, until he was asked what troubled him. He rose up and said: "I've been a fool on this tariff question all my days, and looking over your mill has let light into my old head. I'll go with you for any fair thing to build more such mills among our farms."

A protective policy binds together all parts of our country as with hooks of steel, and helps to good work and good will for all.

CHAPTER XIII.

OUR HISTORY TEACHES THE BENEFITS OF PROTECTION.

Our national history teaches the benefits of protection and the perils of free trade. Within three months after his inauguration as our first President, Washington readily signed the first tariff act, "for the encouragement and protection of manufactures." Jefferson and other leading men held like opinions, and Fisher Ames, of Massachusetts, said in Congress, in the debates on the first tariff bill: "The present Constitution was dictated by commercial necessity more than any other cause. The want of an efficient government to secure our manufacturing interest and advance our commerce was long seen by men of judgment and patriots." No marvel in this, since Great Britain constantly crushed our commerce and manufactures by oppressive laws, so long as we were her subject colonies. Yet to-day men in Congress and elsewhere profess to doubt what no man of any party doubted then,—the Constitutional right to enact protective tariff laws, a right maintained by the words and acts of Hamilton, Madison and other framers of our Constitution. Modern free traders claim to know what that instrument means better than its framers. Theorists like Professor Perry arraign the wisdom of these great men, and assert that they established an "utterly false principle" in "national legislation," which has grown "more unjust and abominable." The protective idea was prominent, too, in the minds of the people. Horace Greeley says (in Political Economy):

"When the Federal Constitution was adopted in 1787, and it was announced that enough States had voted to ratify it, there were instantly great rejoicings in all the seaboard villages, and great processions were formed, wherein the laboring classes appeared parading the hammer and the anvil, crying out, 'Protection to American industry!' They had had free trade since the war ended, and they had had enough of markets glutted with foreign goods and no demand for American labor."

He states, also, that when a protective tariff act was passed in 1828, the British vessels in Charleston harbor put their flags at half mast as mourning over a calamity.

But the early protective measures were inadequate, although beneficial to some extent.

At the close of the war of 1812 the country was overwhelmed by the enormous importation of cottons and woolens, admitted at a duty of five per cent. *ad valorem.* Although Great Britain lost heavily by the first importations, she consoled herself for this loss by the prospect of permanently commanding our markets. It was at this very period, namely, on the 9th of April, 1816, that Mr. Brougham remarked in the House of Commons:

"It was well worth while to incur a loss upon the first exportation, in order, by the glut, to stifle in the cradle those infant manufactures in the United States, which the war had forced into existence, contrary to the natural order of things."

Mr. Greeley gives his personal recollections as follows:

"My distinct personal recollections on this head go back to the period of industrial derangement, business collapse, and widespread pecuniary ruin, which followed the close, in 1815, of our last war with Great Britain. Peace found this country dotted with furnaces and factories, which had suddenly sprung up under the precarious shelter of embargo and war. These—not yet firmly established, in a country whose commerce, before canals, railroads or steam were known, was almost wholly external or on the seaboard—found themselves suddenly exposed to a determined and relentless foreign competition. Great Britain had pushed her fabrics into almost every corner of the world. Of some of these great stocks had nevertheless accumulated, out of fashion, and only salable far below cost. These were thrown on our markets in a perfect deluge, being advertised in Boston journals at 'pound for pound,' —that is, what cost $4.44 (really $4.80) to make in England being sold in Boston, duty and charges paid, for $3.33. The tariff of 1816, mainly framed by William Lowndes, was meant as a barrier against this inundation, but proved inadequate, except on coarse cottons and a few other rude products. Our manufactories went down like grain before the mower; our agriculture and the wages of labor speedily followed. In New England I judge that fully one-fourth of the property went through the sheriff's mill; and the prostration was scarcely less general elsewhere. In Kentucky the presence of debt was universal and intolerable. In New York the principal merchants united (1817) in a memorial to Congress to save our commerce as well as our manufactures from utter ruin by increasing the tariff and prohibiting the sale at auction of imported fabrics."

The tariff act of 1816 extended and increased specific duties, and was passed by a vote of 88 to 54 in the House and a majority in the Senate. Twenty-five votes in its favor were cast by Southern members, such eminent men as Lumpkins and Cuthbert of Georgia, R. M. Johnson of Kentucky, Barbour and St. George Tucker of Virginia, and Lowndes and John C. Calhoun of South Carolina, among them,—the last named strongly advocating the measure as necessary for prosperity and national unity.

But these able men, build up our manufactures and thus benefit ou...ns, had not learned the persistent resolve and power of our British competitors, and the tariff they framed, although protective in its aim and method, did not prove to be a barrier strong enough, and a few years showed that it must be strengthened, as it was by the tariff of 1824.

The Chicago *Commercial Advertiser* sums up later tariff history as follows:

"Our first tariff worthy of the name of protection was that of 1824. For a number of years previous to that date the condition of the whole country was deplorable. The American markets were flooded with foreign merchandise. Home manufacturers were everywhere overmastered by ruinous competition from abroad. Employment was scarce and wages ridiculously low. An embarrassed condition was the common lot. So soon as the tariff of 1824 went into operation the whole aspect and course of affairs were changed. Activity took the place of sluggishness. Capital sought investments. Labor came into demand. Wages advanced. Mines were opened, furnaces built, mills started, shops multiplied. Business revived in all its departments. Revenue flowed copiously into the coffers of the government. The debts created by two expensive wars were entirely paid off. Such a scene of general prosperity had never before been seen by our people. More stringent protection was provided by the act of 1828, and affairs still more rapidly improved. President Jackson said, in his annual message, December 4, 1832: 'Our country presents on every side marks of prosperity and happiness, unequaled, perhaps, in any other portion of the world.'

"Then came the nullification times of South Carolina and the compromise tariff of 1833. This act took effect January 1, 1834, and was to operate by a series of periodical reductions of the rates on imports until June 30, 1842, after which date no duty was to exceed twenty per cent. Under this legislation industry and trade soon declined. Foreign goods poured like an inundation into our markets. Less than three and a half years brought the panic and the collapse of 1837. Affairs went from bad to worse. The government became impoverished with the people. Its resources sank so low that President Tyler could not at one time obtain the payment of his salary, and had to resort to the brokers for loans.

"Alleviation was sought and obtained by the protective tariff of 1842, the best measure of the kind we have had in all our history.

A most extraordinary revival of production and trade was speedily accomplished. We may sum up the results in the words of President Polk's annual message, December 8, 1846, as follows: 'Labor in all its branches is receiving an ample reward, while education, science, and the arts are rapidly enlarging the means of social happiness. The progress of our country in her career of greatness, not only in the vast extension of our territorial limits, and in the rapid increase of our population, but in resources and wealth, and in the happy condition of our people, is without an example in the history of nations.'

"When these glowing words were published the free trade tariff of 1846 had been in operation just eight days. Although the movement was slower than from 1833, the decadence went on steadily. Our Presidents ceased to congratulate the country on its prosperity. Yet a further reduction of the tariff took place in 1857, followed, in a few months, by the panic of that year. Revenue declined. Wages went down. Employment at any pay was hard to find. Just before the rebellion the government was borrowing money to pay its ordinary expenses in time of peace.

"In 1861 was passed that protective tariff which the free traders denounced as 'the bill of abominations.' Under that and the following acts we once more had a marvelous recuperation of production and commerce."

With comprehensive terseness Henry C. Carey condenses the matter in this way ·

"Protection, as established in 1813, 1828, 1842, gave, as that of 1861 is giving: Great demand for labor. Wages high and money cheap. Public and private revenues large, and immigration great and steadily increasing. Public and private property great beyond all previous precedent. Growing national independence."

"British free trade as established in 1817, 1834, 1846 and 1857, bequeathed to its successor: Labor everywhere seeking to be employed. Wages low and money high. Public and private revenues small and steadily decreasing. Immigration declining. Public and private bankruptcy nearly universal. Growing national dependence."

PROTECTIVE TARIFFS BEST FOR REVENUE.

The *Chicago Morning Herald* refutes a loose assertion of the *Chicago Tribune* that "tariffs are a mechanism for promoting protection by choking off revenue," by a tabular statement of receipts in fifteen years of revenue tariffs, from 1847 to 1861, as $708,082,956,—and for fifteen years with a protective tariff, from 1867 to 1881, as $2,577,601,931,—the revenue for government in the last, or protective, period, *three and a half times greater than in the tariff for revenue period!*

Not forgetful of the effects of good or bad crops, of wars, and of the new abundance of gold and silver in the world, we can see that our protective policy has been a power for good through all. It should be borne especially in mind that the panic and financial peril of the last few years, beginning in the United States in 1873, was world-wide; was the only panic ever felt in this country under a protective policy; and that we felt it less, had less distress of workmen and disaster to capital than free-trade England, and recovered from it sooner than England did. France, a protective country, and the United States with a like policy, had less trouble and earlier recovery than any other great nations. The horizontal reduction of ten per cent. in our tariff in 1872, doubtless helped to increase the panic of 1873.

The credit of our government, and the interest it pays on its notes and bonds, tells the same story. In 1860, at the close of a dozen years of revenue tariff, treasury notes payable in one year were issued as a necessity to pay expenses. Of these $10,000,000 worth were sold with some difficulty, half of them at 12 per cent., over three-fourths at 10 to 12 per cent., one-tenth only at 6 to 8 per cent.,—high rates for those days. Now our government pays low rates, 3 or 4 per cent. as a sure investment for hundreds of millions of capital.

COOPER INSTITUTE SPEECH, IN NEW YORK, OF DEXTER A. HAWKINS.

A great meeting was held February 1st, 1883, in the Cooper Institute, at which Peter Cooper presided, and Hon. W. M. Evarts and other eminent men spoke. Extracts from the address of Mr. Hawkins will help our knowledge of the industrial history we are now making :

"We have had four protective tariffs in this century. Under the three former the country was uniformly prosperous. Immediately following their respective repeals, the country passed through periods of great depression, insolvency, and bankruptcy. But, as the nation was then small and poor, the free traders may say that what was for our interest then is not for our interest now,—that we are so large and prosperous that a different system is required.

"Let us consider, then, the effect upon the prosperity of the country of the tariff of 1861, which is now in force. This prosperity, like a river, is made up of many streamlets.

"The mining and consumption of coal means force, power, energy for manufactures, transportation, and the creation of wealth. England now mines one hundred and sixty million tons of coal a year. This applied to her machinery gives her the producing and wealth-creating capacity of six hundred millions of men, though her population is less than forty millions.

"In 1861 our output of coal was only sixteen million tons. In 1882, after twenty-one years of protective tariff, it had risen to ninety million tons, being a gain of four hundred and sixty-two and a half per cent. That means that the effective capacity of the machinery of this country and its power to create wealth are five and five-eighths times what they were twenty-one years ago.

"Twenty years more of like progress and our output of coal

will exceed that of England or any other country on the globe, and will give us a capacity in producive machinery of at least six hundred millions of human beings.

"A high protective tariff is a sort of Titanic steam-pressure put upon this enormous dormant force of wealth and influence to make it active and productive.

"In 1861 we had only thirty-one thousand miles of railway, and nearly all of this was single track. Now we have one hundred and fourteen thousand miles, one-quarter of which is double track, being a gain in mileage, under the stimulus of twenty-one years of protective tariff, of eighty-three thousand miles, or two hundred and thirty-seven per cent. The value of this eighty-three thousand miles, at the average capitalization of fifty thousand dollars per mile, is four thousand one hundred and fifty millions ($4,150,000,000). This is just so much, in this item alone, added to our national wealth in this short period.

"The gross earnings of this hundred and fourteen thousand miles of railway, last year, were eight hundred million dollars ($800,000,000), or an average of seven thousand dollars per mile; and yet transportation of freight and passengers has been cheapened, until now it is only one-quarter of what it was thirty years ago.

"*The gross earnings last year of our railways were sufficient to buy the entire mercantile marine of Great Britain.*
*   *   *   *   *   *   *   *   *

"A tariff, protecting our own industry against injurious foreign competition, compels foreign countries to send us, instead of merchandise, their operatives, to save them from starvation, and their capitalists in order to find profitable employment for their money. If we let their merchandise come in without protective taxation, these operatives and capitalists would eke out a subsistence at home, and their countries would send us merchandise instead of men and women.

"European statisticians inform us that the average cost to them of raising the emigrants that come to this country is one thousand dollars per head. They are worth to us much more than that sum." *   *   *   *   *   *

"Are we now prepared to try the disastrous experiment of free trade for the fifth time?

"We have been doing very well, under a protective tariff. Hadn't we better let well enough alone?

"Modifications in detail are required, but the principle of protection to our own industries is sound and should not be touched, for it leads only to individual and national prosperity."

The *New York Shipping List* says that forty-two years ago the wealth of Great Britain was computed to be five fold greater than ours, but now Mr. Mulhall, an eminent English statistician, concedes that the United States exceeds Great Britain in total wealth, though not quite equal to it *per capita.*

Estimates made by Charles S. Hill, Statistician of the Department of State, representing the Metropolitan Industrial League, of New York, which appear in evidence taken by the tariff commission, are as follows:

Population.—United States, 50,150,000; Great Britain, 34,505,000; France, 37,166,000; Germany, 45,367,000; Russia, 82,400,000; Austria, 39,175,000.

Wealth.—United States, $55,000,000,000; Great Britain, $45,000,000,000; France, $40,000,000,000; Germany, $25,000,000,000; Russia, $15,000,000,000; Austria, $14,000,000,000.

This chapter of lessons from our history has a solid value, not to be found in any plausible free trade theories. Those theories are like apples of Sodom—fair to the eye, but nauseous to the taste.

CHAPTER XIV.

FOREIGN COMMERCE—AMERICAN SHIPS.

"Of what consequence is it to me whose ships sail from our ports? British or American, it affects me little if any." Something like this the farmer on a Western prairie, or the cotton grower far up some Southern river, might say. Yet it is very important to them. Let war break out in Europe, and Great Britain be involved, while British ships carry our wheat and cotton and provisions, and a blockade rolls back a tide of disaster to every farmer's door, no matter how far inland he may be. Let American ships be our carriers, and our flag, at peace with all Europe, conveys those farm products safe to every land. American ships must carry our exports to foreign countries, and none are more interested in this than our farmers. The manufacturer has like interest, for the same reason, and also because foreign ship-owners cannot be expected to help him in getting good markets as Americans would. On the seas, as on land, we want an American policy—the control of our trade and transportation—and for this we must build up a great American commercial marine.

At an early day, when only a narrow line along our Atlantic coast was settled, and the development of the great West was hardly thought of, the ocean opened a wide field for enterprise, the troubled condition of European affairs favored our ships, and a large ocean carrying trade fell into our hands. Then came the rapid settlement of the West, the period of internal development, with capital and enterprise turning westward instead of oceanward, railroads built at a cost greater than that of the whole British navy, farms, factories, towns and cities springing up in the wilderness and on the prairies, thousands of steamers and sail vessels built to carry on our vast inland commerce, greater than all our foreign trade. In the late civil war British Alabamas in Confederate service swept our seas and crippled our merchant ships. The new era of iron ship building began in England, and Great Britain spent millions yearly in paying for ocean mail service which extended her trade over the world, and our foreign shipping was fearfully crippled. It has not been built up for two reasons. The great work of internal development still goes on, *the railroad pays better than the ship*, mines and farms wait to be opened, and to pay well for opening, and so capital goes landward and not oceanward. Meanwhile the policy of our government toward our foreign shipping has been blindly unjust and absurd. But the time has come when it is highly important that we should be our own carriers, on sea as on land, and so be able to extend our trade and increase our exports, especially of manufactures. It appears that in 1860 fifty-nine per cent. of the French foreign trade was in foreign ships; in 1880, seventy per cent. Germany, Italy and Spain show like results; but ours is the poorest showing of all, being from twenty-nine to eighty-two per cent. in the same time. France is aroused, and is paying millions yearly for ocean mail service. Surely we should adopt a wiser policy than that of our past twenty years.

Our ship-builders and owners ask that the American ship shall be taxed as little as the British ship is, and shall be decently paid for ocean mail-carrying, instead of being compelled to carry mails at less than a tenth of what coasting vessels, those on inland waters, and railroads get for like service. England pays yearly some $4,000,000 to her vessels for carrying foreign mails all over the world, taxes them far less than we do ours, and thus builds up a trade of hundreds of millions yearly, and gets some $200,000,000 for freight, of which we pay $100,000,000.

France pays a bounty to her home-built ships. In opposition to any justice to our shipping, and thus to our country at large, the senseless cry of "free ships" and "subsidies" is heard,—the echo of a voice that speaks from British counting-rooms and ship-yards.

The difference in taxation is tersely stated by John Roach, of New York, as follows:

"Suppose five 4,000-ton steamers had been given to a company of free-ship men for nothing in 1865, the value of the ships being $5,000,000. The account at the end of a year would stand thus between them and their English competitors:

Taxation of American line on its $5,000,-
000 of property at 2¼ per cent........$125,000
Wages, 600 men for the 5 ships, at $2
per day........................... 438,000 .

Total taxation and running expenses
American line........................$563,000

Interest on $5,000,000 capital, English
line, at 4 per cent..................$200,000
Taxation, 1 per cent., on net earnings,
say earning 6 per cent.............. 3,000
Wages, 600 men, $1.25 per day........ 273,750

Total running expenses English line........$476,750

Difference in favor of English line........ $86,250

"Here is an advantage of $86,250 a year when the Americans were given their ships for nothing, and no account is taken of interest on capital. And since the Americans who wanted free ships, or said they did, could not expect to get them for nothing, how would they have stood in the competition when they had bought them?"

The absurd injustice of our government in the matter of foreign mail carriage is forcibly shown by the fact that lines of ships in our coasting trade carry mails 247,960 miles for $142,766, while ships in foreign trade carry mails 1,181,309 miles for only $31,405,—our coasting ships being paid $57\frac{1}{4}$ cents per mile, our ships in foreign trade only two and a half cents. In contrast with this strange injustice Great Britain, from 1840 to 1880, paid $240,000,000 to her ships in foreign trade for mail carriage. Propose anything of the kind here and the cry of "subsidy" is raised. From 1872 to 1882 we built in this country 260,000 tons of coasting steam vessels, mostly iron, or more than all the steam-tonnage of England in 1860, and these vessels, many of them large and fine, have reduced the rates of coasting freight nearly 50 per cent. since 1870.

This shows our ability to build ships, and they are equal to any in the world. Mr. Roach says:

"We have no difficulty in raising capital to be put into large American-built ocean steamers for the coasting trade, where it will be subject to the same laws, rates, and taxation as the other capital employed in that trade. But when we undertake to put capital into the foreign trade, we bring it into competition with the capital of other peoples, who have more favorable conditions of interest, taxation, and labor, and there we find the hunt for capital a vain one. The only way to get it is for our government to pursue the same policy that England did when she was in a like condition (and does still)—encourage capital to invest by opening up new markets through the establishment of mail steamship lines. Moreover, we urgently need these new markets, and there is no other means except superior facilities of communication (mail and passenger), whereby we can obtain them."

This important subject can only be briefly treated, but its great and vital importance—especially to the growers of grain and cotton, and the producer of provisions—calls for these few suggestive facts. We should become our own ocean carriers to a far greater extent than we are, and to that end *we must build and control our own shipping*, as England does hers, and as every great and independent commercial nation must. In 1881 our exports were *eleven million tons;* in 1890 they may reach *fifty million tons*. By a wise policy we can carry a goodly share of this vast tonnage in American ships at no higher rates than we now pay to foreigners,—probably lower,—and thus keep over $100,000,000 in freight expenses at home each year, and help our country in other ways.

CONCLUSION.

My task is done. The facts and statements of this work have been gathered and presented with patient care and arduous labor. That labor has been lightened by a sense of the justice and wisdom of the principles and the policy advocated, and by a hope that it might help to a better understanding of a subject of great interest and importance. Guided by experience, we may well avoid the shallow fallacies of free trade or the disaster of a tariff for revenue only, and persist firmly in protection to American industry; thus realizing material prosperity, national unity, and the well being of the people.

www.ingramcontent.com/pod-product-compliance
Lightning Source LLC
Chambersburg PA
CBHW021732220426
43662CB00008B/822